Corinne Keller

Freiarbeitsmaterialien für die 6. Klasse: Englisch

alle grammatischen Schwerpunkte –
drei Differenzierungsstufen – flexibel einsetzbar

Corinne Keller arbeitet als Englisch- und Deutschlehrerin an einer Realschule in Baden-Württemberg und ist zudem als LRS-Beauftragte und Fortbildnerin tätig. Bei ihrer Arbeit mit Kindern ist es ihr wichtig, die Kinder differenziert und individuell zu fördern. Durch ihre langjährigen Erfahrungen im Förderbereich und durch ihre Ausbildung zur Systemischen Beraterin weiß sie um die vielfältigen Bedürfnisse von Kindern beim Lernen.

Wir haben unseren Markennamen von scolix zu scolix geändert. Alle Inhalte entsprechen den bisher unter dem Namen scolix erschienenen Auflagen.

Wir verwenden in unseren Werken eine genderneutrale Sprache, damit sich alle gleichermaßen angesprochen fühlen. Wenn keine neutrale Formulierung möglich ist, nennen wir die weibliche und die männliche Form. In Fällen, in denen wir aufgrund einer besseren Lesbarkeit nur ein Geschlecht nennen können, achten wir darauf, den unterschiedlichen Geschlechtsidentitäten gleichermaßen gerecht zu werden.

In diesem Werk sind nach dem MarkenG geschützte Marken und sonstige Kennzeichen für eine bessere Lesbarkeit nicht besonders kenntlich gemacht. Es kann also aus dem Fehlen eines entsprechenden Hinweises nicht geschlossen werden, dass es sich um einen freien Warennamen handelt.

4. Auflage 2025
© 2015 scolix Verlag, Hamburg

AAP Lehrerwelt GmbH
Veritaskai 3
21079 Hamburg
Telefon: +49 (0) 40325083-040
E-Mail: info@lehrerwelt.de
Geschäftsführung: Andrea Fischer, Sandra Saghbazarian
USt-ID: DE 173 77 61 42
Register: AG Hamburg HRB/126335
Alle Rechte vorbehalten.

Das Werk als Ganzes sowie in seinen Teilen unterliegt dem deutschen Urheberrecht. Die Erwerbenden einer Einzellizenz des Werkes sind berechtigt, das Werk als Ganzes oder in seinen Teilen für den eigenen Gebrauch und den Einsatz im eigenen Präsenz- wie auch dem Distanzunterricht zu nutzen. Produkte, die aufgrund ihres Bestimmungszweckes zur Vervielfältigung und Weitergabe zu Unterrichtszwecken gedacht sind (insbesondere Kopiervorlagen und Arbeitsblätter), dürfen zu Unterrichtszwecken vervielfältigt und weitergegeben werden.

Die Nutzung ist nur für den genannten Zweck gestattet, nicht jedoch für einen schulweiten Einsatz und Gebrauch, für die Weiterleitung an Dritte einschließlich weiterer Lehrkräfte, für die Veröffentlichung im Internet oder in (Schul-)Intranets oder einen weiteren kommerziellen Gebrauch. Mit dem Kauf einer Schullizenz ist die Schule berechtigt, die Inhalte durch alle Lehrkräfte des Kollegiums der erwerbenden Schule sowie durch die Schülerinnen und Schüler der Schule und deren Eltern zu nutzen.

Nicht erlaubt ist die Weiterleitung der Inhalte an Lehrkräfte, Schülerinnen und Schüler, Eltern, andere Personen, soziale Netzwerke, Downloaddienste oder Ähnliches außerhalb der eigenen Schule.
Eine über den genannten Zweck hinausgehende Nutzung bedarf in jedem Fall der vorherigen schriftlichen Zustimmung des Verlags. Sind Internetadressen in diesem Werk angegeben, wurden diese vom Verlag sorgfältig geprüft. Da wir auf die externen Seiten weder inhaltliche noch gestalterische Einflussmöglichkeiten haben, können wir nicht garantieren, dass die Inhalte zu einem späteren Zeitpunkt noch dieselben sind wie zum Zeitpunkt der Drucklegung. Der scolix Verlag übernimmt deshalb keine Gewähr für die Aktualität und den Inhalt dieser Internetseiten oder solcher, die mit ihnen verlinkt sind, und schließt jegliche Haftung aus.

Die automatisierte Analyse des Werkes, um daraus Informationen insbesondere über Muster, Trends und Korrelationen gemäß § 44b UrhG („Text und Data Mining") zu gewinnen, ist untersagt.

Autorschaft:	Corinne Keller
Redaktion:	Redaktion: Kathrin Roth)
Covergestaltung:	TSA&B Werbeagentur GmbH, Hamburg
Coverfoto:	AAP Lehrerwelt GmbH
Illustrationen:	© Corinne Keller
Satz:	Satzpunkt Ursula Ewert GmbH, Bayreuth
Druck und Bindung:	SDK Systemdruck GmbH, Köln

ISBN: 978-3-403-10302-8
www.scolix.de

Inhaltsverzeichnis

Vorwort	4
Wie arbeite ich mit den Aufgabenblättern?	5
Revision: Simple Present – Positive and negative statements – Activity: Tandem	6
Revision: Simple Present – Questions – Activity: Tandem	7
Revision: Present Progressive – Positive and negative statements – Activity: Tandem	8
Revision: Present progressive – Questions – Activity: Tandem	9
Simple Past – Positive forms of (to) be: "was" / "were"	10
Simple Past – Negative forms of (to) be: "was not" / "were not"	13
Simple Past – Short forms of (to) be – Negative forms: "wasn't" / "weren't"	16
Simple Past – Questions with (to) be: "Was …?" / "Were …?"	19
Simple Past – Short answers with (to) be: "was / wasn't" and "were / weren't"	22
Simple Past forms of (to) be – Activity: Tandem	25
Simple Past – Questions with (to) be: question word + "was" / "were"	26
Simple Past – Positive statements with regular verbs ("verb-ed")	29
Simple Past – Positive statements with irregular verbs	30
Simple Past – Spelling – Activity: Sorting	32
Simple Past and adverbs of frequency – Activity: Cutting out	33
Simple Past – Negative statements with "didn't"	34
Simple Past – Questions with "did"	35
Simple Past – Questions and short answers with "did"	38
Simple Past – Questions with question words	40
Simple Past – Questions ending with a preposition	43
Possessive pronouns	46
Present Perfect – Positive statements with regular verbs ("verb-ed")	48
Present Perfect – Positive statements with irregular verbs	49
Present Perfect and adverbs of frequency – Activity: Cutting out	51
Present Perfect – Negative statements	52
Present Perfect – Questions with "Have …?" / "Has …?"	54
Present Perfect – Questions and short answers with "have" / "has"	57
Present Perfect – Questions with question words	59
Question tags	62
The going to-future – Positive statements	63
The going to-future – Negative statements (long form)	66
The going to-future – Negative statements (short form)	69
The going to-future – Questions	72
The will-future	75
The will-future: Questions with "Will …?"	78
The will-future: Short answers – Activity: Tandem	81
Conditional sentences type I with "will"	82
Adjectives – The comparison of adjectives	85
Past Progressive – Positive statements	88
Past Progressive – Spelling	91
Past Progressive – Negative statements (long form) with "was not / were not"	92
Past Progressive – Negative statements (short form) with "wasn't / weren't"	95
Past Progressive – Questions with "Was …?" / "Were …?"	98
Past Progressive – Questions with question words	101
Simple Past and Past Progressive	104
Adverbs and Adjectives	109
Adverbs – Special forms and spelling – Activity: Sorting	112

Vorwort

Liebe Kolleginnen und Kollegen,

mit diesem Buch *Freiarbeitsmaterial für die 6. Klasse: Englisch* halten Sie Übungsmaterial in Händen, das fast den gesamten Stoff der sechsten Jahrgangsstufe abdeckt. Dieses Freiarbeitsmaterial ist in der schulischen Praxis entstanden und wurde gezielt für die schulische Praxis konzipiert. Deshalb habe ich besonders großen Wert auf die folgenden Aspekte gelegt:

Direkte Einsetzbarkeit

Oftmals scheitert der Einsatz von Freiarbeitsmaterial schon daran, dass umfangreiche Vorbereitungsarbeiten die Lehrkraft abschrecken. Dies wurde hier insofern berücksichtigt, als Sie zur Vorbereitung lediglich das Material in Klassenstärke kopieren und die Schüler einmal in die Arbeit damit einweisen müssen.

Material zu allen grundlegenden Themen

Das Heft bietet Ihnen umfangreiches Freiarbeitsmaterial für alle wichtigen Grammatikthemen der 6. Klasse.

Einheitliche Systematik

Wenn Sie dieses umfassende Angebot häufiger einsetzen, sind die Schüler schnell vertraut mit Aufbau und Aufgabenformat der Materialien, wodurch Sie weniger Zeit für Instruktionen und Anweisungen aufwenden müssen.

Differenzierung

Um jeden Schüler seinem Leistungsstand entsprechend zu fördern, liegen die Aufgaben jeweils in drei unterschiedlichen Schwierigkeitsgraden vor. Die leichtere Variante ist mit einem Stern gekennzeichnet. Sie enthält einfachere Aufgaben und minimiert zusätzlich bei Schreibaufgaben deren Umfang, während die anspruchsvolleren Aufgaben mit zwei bzw. drei Sternen höhere Anforderungen an die Schüler stellen. Da diese Symbole in allen Bänden dieser Reihe vorkommen, ist der Wiedererkennungswert sehr hoch; sie sind den Schülern schnell vertraut.

Spielerische Lernformen

An verschiedenen Stellen werden spielerische Lernformate wie Dominos, Puzzles oder Tandems eingesetzt, da gerade diese Übungsformen ein soziales Lernen ermöglichen, das eine aktive Wissenskonstruktion der Schüler unterstützt und dabei hoch motivierend ist.

Selbsttätigkeit / Selbstkorrektur

Besonders effektiv wirkt sich der Einsatz dieses Materials aus, wenn Schüler die eigenen Lösungen selbstständig vergleichen. Die Aufgaben sind so angelegt, dass die Selbstkontrolle schnell und einfach gelingt. Dies entlastet nicht nur Sie, sodass Sie verstärkt in die Rolle des Beraters schlüpfen können, sondern führt darüber hinaus dazu, dass Schüler die eigenen Lösungswege überdenken. Trainieren Sie Ihren Schülern das eigenständige Verbessern der Aufgaben frühzeitig an und weisen Sie sie immer wieder auf die Wichtigkeit der Selbstkorrektur hin.

Für dieses Material bieten sich vor allem diese zwei unterschiedlichen Einsatzmöglichkeiten an:
1. In einem Ordner im Klassenzimmer als Freiarbeitsmaterial zur Verfügung gestellt, ermöglicht es schnelleren Schülern, die Wartezeit sinnvoll zu nutzen, wenn sie mit den gestellten Aufgaben bereits vor ihren Klassenkameraden fertig sind.
2. In der Vorbereitung auf Leistungsfeststellungen kann das Freiarbeitsmaterial als Lernzirkel eingesetzt werden und ermöglicht so den Schülern, das gesamte Stoffgebiet zu wiederholen und Lücken zu schließen.

Ich wünsche Ihnen und Ihren Schülern freudvolles, erfolgreiches Lernen mit den folgenden Arbeitsmaterialien.

Wie arbeite ich mit den Aufgabenblättern?

1. Überschrift lesen	Die Überschrift verrät dir, welches Thema behandelt wird.
2. Schwierigkeitsgrad beachten	Die Anzahl der Sterne zeigt dir an, ob die Übungen dazu leichter oder schwieriger sind. ☆ steht dabei für die Erarbeitung von Grundlagen bzw. Aufgaben, die leichter zu lösen sind ☆☆ stehen dafür, dass die Übungen umfangreicher sind und an Schwierigkeit zunehmen ☆☆☆ stehen dafür, dass diese Übungen kniffliger sind Du kannst bei Themen, die dir schwerfallen, natürlich erst mit einem Stern beginnen und dich zu einem späteren Zeitpunkt an den anderen Sternchen-Aufgaben versuchen.
3. Aufgabenstellung lesen und Beispiel anschauen	Bevor du mit einer Übung beginnst, lies dir immer erst die Aufgabenstellung durch und schau dir das Beispiel und die Hilfen wie Symbole und Merkkästen dazu genau an. Manchmal helfen dir auch Linien und Pfeile dabei, eine Aufgabe besser zu verstehen.
4. Lösungen nach hinten falten	Jedes Arbeitsblatt hat eine Lösung. Diese musst du entweder nach hinten falten, umdrehen oder durch ein Lösungswort überprüfen. Es macht wenig Sinn, die Lösungen abzuschreiben, nur weil sie auf dem Arbeitsblatt zu finden sind. Damit betrügst du dich nur selbst. Klappe daher die Lösungen nach hinten oder decke sie ab und schaue erst nach, wenn du fertig bist, oder eine kurze Hilfestellung benötigst.
5. Activity-Übungen	Dies sind Aufgaben, für die du manchmal zusätzlich eine Schere und Klebstoff brauchst, manchmal auch einen Partner.

Revision: Simple Present – Positive and negative statements – Activity: Tandem

Work with a partner. Fold the paper. One of you is partner A and the other is partner B. Partner A gives the answer (long form) for each gap. Partner B checks the answers. Then it's partner B's turn and partner A checks the answers.

Positive and negative sentences in the Simple Present	Answers: Positive and negative sentences in the Simple Present
Partner A	**Partner B**
a) I _____ (go) to school every day.	a) I *go* to school every day.
b) He ___ (not like) to do homework.	b) He *does not like* to do homework.
c) They usually ___ (play) football after school.	c) They usually *play* football after school.
d) Linda _____ (be) my best friend.	d) Linda *is* my best friend.
e) Peter _____ (not be) in Year 7.	e) Peter *is not* in Year 7.
f) It always _____ (rain) a lot in autumn.	f) It always *rains* a lot in autumn.
g) Lara _____ (not see) her friends every day.	g) Lara *does not see* her friends every day.
h) You _____ (be) too early!	h) You *are* too early!
i) Peter and Lynn _____ (like) old movies.	i) Peter and Lynn *like* old movies.
j) My friends _____ (not like) dancing at parties.	j) My friends *do not like* dancing at parties.
k) We _____ (not be) at home.	k) We *are not* at home.

Answers: Positive and negative sentences in the Simple Present	Positive and negative sentences in the Simple Present
Partner A	**Partner B**
a) Tom *knows* a lot about dogs.	a) Tom _____ (know) a lot about dogs.
b) We *are* best friends.	b) We _____ (be) best friends.
c) My friends *do not go* dancing every night.	c) My friends _____ (not go) dancing every night.
d) I often *have* dinner with my dad.	d) I often _____ (have) dinner with my dad.
e) It *is* hot outside.	e) It _____ (be) hot outside.
f) My father *does not like* his new job.	f) My father _____ (not like) his new job.
g) It *is not* cold here.	g) It _____ (not be) cold here.
h) Tom always *has* fun at school.	h) Tom always _____ (have) fun at school.
i) Peter and Tom *work* on Saturdays.	i) Peter and Tom _____ (work) on Saturdays.
j) Her friend *does not live* in Berlin.	j) Her friend _____ (not live) in Berlin.
k) I *do not wear* shorts in winter.	k) I _____ (not wear) shorts in winter.

Revision: Simple Present – Questions – Activity: Tandem

Work with a partner. Fold the paper. One of you is partner A and the other is partner B. Partner A gives the answer for each gap. Partner B checks the answers. Then it's partner B's turn and partner A checks the answers.

Questions in the Simple Present	Answers: Questions in the Simple Present
Partner A	**Partner B**
a) Where _____ (you / live)?	a) Where *do you live*?
b) Which film _____ (he / like) the best?	b) Which film *does he like* the best?
c) Whose jacket _____ (be) this?	c) Whose jacket *is* this?
d) Why _____ (he / know) so much about dogs?	d) Why *does he know* so much about dogs?
e) How often _____ (you / play) football?	e) How often *do you play* football?
f) What _____ (be) your favourite colours?	f) What *are* your favourite colours?
g) How long _____ (you / sleep) every day?	g) How long *do you sleep* every day?
h) How much _____ (it / cost)?	h) How much *does it cost*?
i) When _____ (she / usually / come) home?	i) When *does she usually come* home?
j) How much _____ (be) these shoes?	j) How much *are* these shoes?
k) Who _____ (Tina / often / talk) to?	k) Who *does Tina often talk* to?

Answers: Questions in the Simple Present	Questions in the Simple Present
Partner A	**Partner B**
a) When *does school start*?	a) When _____ (school / start)?
b) How many times *do you practise* every day?	b) How many times ___ (you / practise) every day?
c) Where *do you go* to school?	c) Where _____ (you / go) to school?
d) Which subject *does Tim like* the best?	d) Which subject _____ (Tim / like) the best?
e) Why *do you like* big dogs?	e) Why _____ (you / like) big dogs?
f) How often *does he play* tennis?	f) How often _____ (he / play) tennis?
g) How long *do your parents work* every day?	g) How long ___ (your parents / work) every day?
h) What *is* your favourite animal?	h) What _____ (be) your favourite animal?
i) How much *does this shirt cost*?	i) How much _____ (this shirt / cost)?
j) Whose shoes *are* these?	j) Whose shoes _____ (be) these?
k) Why *do you like* Maths so much?	k) Why _____ (you / like) Maths so much?

Revision: Present Progressive – Positive and negative statements – Activity: Tandem

Work with a partner. Fold the paper. One of you is partner A and the other is partner B. Partner A gives the answer (long form) for each gap. Partner B checks the answers. Then it's partner B's turn and partner A checks the answers.

Negative and positive sentences in the Present Progressive	Answers: Negative and positive sentences in the Present Progressive
Partner A	**Partner B**
a) Look! It _____ (rain) right now.	a) Look! It *is raining* right now.
b) He _____ (sleep) at the moment.	b) He *is sleeping* at the moment.
c) They _____ (not work) right now.	c) They *are not working* right now.
d) Listen! She _____ (not play) the piano anymore.	d) Listen! She *is not playing* the piano anymore.
e) I _____ (wait) for him this morning.	e) I *am waiting* for him this morning.
f) Look! My sister _____ (not have) lunch.	f) Look! My sister *is not having* lunch.
g) At the moment he _____ (not work).	g) At the moment he *is not working.*
h) The cat _____ (sit) on the sofa right now.	h) The cat *is sitting* on the sofa right now.
i) The dog _____ (not bark) at the moment.	i) The dog *is not barking* at the moment.
j) I _____ (not buy) this book today.	j) I *am not buying* this book today.
k) He _____ (go) to the cinema this evening.	k) He *is going* to the cinema this evening.
Answers: Negative and positive sentences in the Present Progressive	**Negative and positive sentences in the Present Progressive**
Partner A	**Partner B**
a) She *is not doing* her homework right now.	a) She _____ (not do) her homework right now.
b) Listen! He *is playing* the drums.	b) Listen! He _____ (play) the drums.
c) At the moment I *am not sleeping*.	c) At the moment I _____ (not sleep).
d) Look! The cats *are not playing* anymore.	d) Look! The cats _____ (not play) anymore.
e) Peter *is repairing* the bike right now.	e) Peter _____ (repair) the bike right now.
f) They *are not going* to the zoo this afternoon.	f) They _____ (not go) to the zoo this afternoon.
g) We *are planning* a trip at the moment.	g) We _____ (plan) a trip at the moment.
h) Tom *is listening* to his new CD just now.	h) Tom _____ (listen) to his new CD just now.
i) Look! It *is not snowing* anymore.	i) Look! It _____ (not snow) anymore.
j) Her mother *is cooking* for us right now.	j) Her mother _____ (cook) for us right now.
k) I *am having* a shower right now.	k) I _____ (have) a shower right now.

Revision: Present Progressive – Questions – Activity: Tandem

Work with a partner. Fold the paper. One of you is partner A and the other is partner B. Partner A gives the answer for each gap. Partner B checks the answers. Then it's partner B's turn and partner A checks the answers.

Questions in the Present Progressive	Answers: Questions in the Present Progressive
Partner A	**Partner B**
a) Listen! Which song _____ (she / sing)?	a) Look! Which song _is she singing_?
b) What _____ (you / do) at the moment?	b) What _are you doing_ at the moment?
c) Look! Where _____ (he / go)?	c) Look! Where _is he going_?
d) Listen! _____ (she / play) the piano?	d) Listen! _Is she playing_ the piano?
e) _____ (they / make) breakfast right now?	e) _Are they making_ breakfast right now?
f) Look! Who _____ (work) in the garden?	f) Look! Who _is working_ in the garden?
g) _____ (she / sleep) at the moment?	g) _Is she sleeping_ at the moment?
h) Where _____ (you / go) now?	h) Where _are you going_ now?
i) Why _____ (the dog / bark) now?	i) Why _is the dog barking_ now?
j) What _____ (she / do) right now?	j) What _is she doing_ right now?
k) Where _____ (you / stay) tonight?	k) Where _are you staying_ tonight?

Answers: Questions in the Present Progressive	Questions in the Present Progressive
Partner A	**Partner B**
a) Why _are you talking_ so fast?	a) Why _____ (you / talk) so fast?
b) Listen! Who _is knocking_ at the door?	b) Listen! Who _____ (knock) at the door?
c) What _is he doing_ here?	c) What _____ (he / do) here?
d) Look! Who _is driving_ that car?	d) Look! Who _____ (drive) that car?
e) Why _are we waiting_ right now?	e) Why _____ (we / wait) right now?
f) Oh no, look! Why _is it starting_ to rain?	f) Oh no, look! Why _____ (it / start) to rain?
g) Listen! What _is the teacher talking_ about?	g) Listen! What _____ (the teacher / talk) about?
h) _Is Peter going_ to the cinema today?	h) _____ (Peter / go) to the cinema today?
i) Which CD _are you listening_ to now?	i) Which CD _____ (you / listen) to now?
j) Whose car _are they cleaning_ right now?	j) Whose car _____ (they / clean) right now?
k) Which movie _are they watching_ now?	k) Which movie _____ (they / watch) now?

Simple Past – Positive forms of (to) be: "was" / "were"

a) Mark the right answer!

Example: We ___ on holiday last week.   ○ was   ● were

●○	a) I ___ at home yesterday.	○ was ○ were	f) Mr Smith ___ our teacher last year.	○ was ○ were	●○
○●	b) They ___ in Spain last year.	○ was ○ were	g) We ___ there last night.	○ was ○ were	○●
●○	c) She ___ here a minute ago.	○ was ○ were	h) The party yesterday ___ great!	○ was ○ were	●○
○●	d) We ___ alone at home yesterday.	○ was ○ were	i) I ___ too late yesterday.	○ was ○ were	●○
○●	e) My parents ___ in Paris last week.	○ was ○ were	j) They ___ in Berlin a month ago.	○ was ○ were	○●

b) Now you! Fill in the right Simple Past form of "be" (was, were):

Example: I <u>was</u> a student.
You <u>were</u> happy.

were	a) Tom and Tim ___ here yesterday.	i) My friends ___ in the park an hour ago.	were
was	b) My friend ___ in France last year.	j) It ___ a great show last night.	was
was	c) Yesterday I ___ very angry.	k) You ___ in the tennis club last year.	were
was	d) My father ___ at home last week.	l) Mr Smith ___ my teacher last year.	was
were	e) Bill and Sue ___ on a trip last May.	m) They ___ in London last week.	were
was	f) It ___ a good party last weekend.	n) I ___ at home last Saturday.	was
were	g) They ___ late last time.	o) It ___ cold outside last week.	was
was	h) It ___ Peter's birthday last week.	p) We ___ too early yesterday.	were

10   Freiarbeitsmaterialien für die 6. Klasse: Englisch

Simple Past – Positive forms of (to) be: "was" / "were"

Form positive statements!
Write down and complete the last part of the first box to form sentences in the Simple Past.

Box 1:
- Here is a piece of Tina's birthday cake. **It**
- Look at all that snow! **There**
- Tom – our cat – broke my glasses. **I**
- I am very tired today. **We**
- Look, there is Peter! **He**
- Did you eat all the chocolate? **It**
- I really miss Amy and Sue! **They**
- This souvenir from Paris is for you. **We**
- ~~We had fun yesterday. It~~
- I am angry at Pit and Tom. **They**
- **There**

Middle box: was / were

Box 2:
- her birthday yesterday.
- a snow storm last night.
- very angry at him yesterday.
- at a disco last night.
- ill last week.
- Tom's chocolate!
- good friends!
- on holiday in France last week.
- ~~a great party.~~
- really late yesterday.
- many people at the concert yesterday.

Example: It   was   a great party.

1. _____
2. _____
3. _____
4. _____
5. _____
6. _____
7. _____
8. _____
9. _____
10. _____

Answers:
1. It was her birthday yesterday.
2. There was a snow storm last night.
3. I was very angry at him yesterday.
4. We were at a disco last night.
5. He was ill last week.
6. It was Tom's chocolate!
7. They were good friends.
8. We were on holiday in France last week.
9. They were really late yesterday.
10. There were many people at the concert yesterday.

Turn over!

Simple Past – Positive forms of (to) be: "was" / "were"

a) Form positive statements. Fill in the right form (was / were):

Last week we _____ in Spain. It _____ great. It _____ hot and sunny. My brother and I _____ at the beach every day. It _____ fantastic and we _____ all happy. It _____ a great holiday. What about you?

We _____ in London. The weather _____ okay. But there _____ many tourists in the city. All the museums and shops _____ full of people. On the last day we _____ at the cinema. The film _____ funny! And what about you?

b) Now you! Where were you on your last holiday?

I _____ _____ . — at home / in Berlin / in Italy / at the beach / …

The weather _____ _____ . — great / hot / sunny / rainy / cold / okay / …

I _____ _____ . — with my family / with my friend(s) / …

It _____ _____ . — great / nice / cool / boring / funny / …

Answers:

Last week we were in Spain. It was great. It was hot and sunny. My brother and I were at the beach every day. It was fantastic and we were all happy. It was a great holiday.
We were in London. The weather was okay. But there were many tourists in the city. All the museums and shops were full of people. On the last day we were at the cinema. The film was funny! We were at the cinema, too. It was a great birthday party.
I was at home with my parents. The weather was great. Last week it was my birthday. We were at the cinema, too. It was a great birthday party.
I was … / The weather was … / I was … / It was …

Simple Past – Negative forms of (to) be: "was not" / "were not"

a) Mark the right answer!

Example: We _____ happy. ○ was not ● were not

● ○	a) I ____ in Berlin last week.	○ was not ○ were not	f) My parents ____ at home last night.	○ was not ○ were not ○ ●
○ ●	b) They ____ angry at him.	○ was not ○ were not	g) Tim and Sue ____ here yesterday.	○ was not ○ were not ○ ●
● ○	c) It ____ his birthday yesterday.	○ was not ○ were not	h) There ____ many people in the shop last Saturday.	○ was not ○ were not ○ ●
● ○	d) Last weekend she ____ at the zoo.	○ was not ○ were not	i) It ____ my idea.	○ was not ○ were not ● ○
● ○	e) Tom ____ at the party last Friday.	○ was not ○ were not	j) We ____ in the USA last month.	○ was not ○ were not ○ ●

b) Form negative statements! Fill in the gaps.

Example: I was happy. → I <u>was</u> <u>not</u> happy.

a)	My father was at home yesterday.	→ My father <u>was</u> _____ at home yesterday.	not
b)	I was alone at home last weekend.	→ I <u>was</u> _____ alone at home last weekend.	not
c)	That was a great party yesterday.	→ That <u>was</u> _____ a great party yesterday.	not
d)	Last night we were at the disco.	→ Last night we <u>were</u> _____ at the disco.	not
e)	He was angry at me.	→ He _____ _____ angry at me.	was not
f)	We were at the market an hour ago.	→ We _____ _____ at the market.	were not
g)	Peter and Sue were here yesterday.	→ Peter and Sue _____ _____ here yesterday.	were not
h)	They were at the cinema last Friday.	→ They _____ _____ at the cinema last Friday.	were not
i)	Tim's party was last weekend.	→ Tim's party _____ _____ last weekend.	was not
j)	He was my teacher last year.	→ He _____ _____ my teacher last year.	was not
k)	John and Tim were in the same class last year.	→ John and Tim _____ _____ in the same class last year.	were not
l)	Jenny was in Year 5 last year.	→ Jenny _____ _____ in Year 5 last year.	was not

Simple Past – Negative forms of (to) be: "was not" / "were not"

a) Form negative statements with "be"! Fill in "was not" or "were not".

Example: I _____ happy. → I <u>was not</u> happy.

was not	a) He _____ in Year 5 last year.	i) Peter and Tim _____ here yesterday.	were not
was not	b) I _____ at Tom's party last Saturday.	j) It _____ my fault!	was not
were not	c) Mum and Dad _____ at home yesterday.	k) John _____ in Berlin last month.	was not
was not	d) Linda _____ at the doctor's last Monday.	l) They _____ tired after the trip.	were not
were not	e) We _____ on holiday last month.	m) She _____ my teacher last year.	was not
was not	f) Tim _____ at home yesterday.	n) Your friends _____ at the concert yesterday.	were not
were not	g) There _____ many people at Tina's last party.	o) The cats _____ hungry.	were not
was not	h) It _____ my dog!	p) Tom _____ on the school trip last Tuesday.	was not

b) Find the right order! Yesterday …

Example: We | not | were | at home → We were not at home.

a) was | happy | I | not → _____ — I was not happy.

b) We | not | were | angry → _____ — We were not angry.

c) They | were | not | here → _____ — They were not here.

d) alone | not | were | We → _____ — We were not alone.

e) I | in Paris | not | was → _____ — I was not in Paris.

f) at school | was | Linda | not → _____ — Linda was not at school.

g) were | The dogs | not | hungry → _____ — The dogs were not hungry.

Simple Past – Negative forms of (to) be: "was not" / "were not"

a) Form negative statements with "be" in the Simple Past! Use "was not" or "were not".

Example: home – I – not be – at → I was not at home yesterday.

a)	here – she – not be – yesterday	→ _____	She was not here yesterday.
b)	in – Pit – not be – Paris – last month	→ _____	Pit was not in Paris last month.
c)	last weekend – not be – we – at the disco	→ _____	Last weekend we were not at the disco.
d)	we – at the cinema – last Friday – not be	→ _____	We were not at the cinema last Friday.
e)	not be – many people – in the shop – there	→ _____	There were not many people in the shop.
f)	I – very happy – not be – yesterday	→ _____	I was not very happy yesterday.
g)	not be – Joe and Tim – last week – at school	→ _____	Joe and Tim were not at school last week.
h)	in my form – Tina – last year – not be	→ _____	Tina was not in my form last year.
i)	not be – angry – mother – my – at him	→ _____	My mother was not angry at him.

b) Find the right order and add "was not" or "were not"!

Example: We | at | home → We | were | not | at | home.

a)	happy	She	very	yesterday	→ _____	She was not very happy yesterday.
b)	my	He	teacher	last year	→ _____	He was not my teacher last year.
c)	birthday	my	last week	It	→ _____	It was not my birthday last week.
d)	yesterday	she	here	→ _____	She was not here yesterday.
e)	We	last month	on	holiday	→ _____	We were not on holiday last month.
f)	yesterday	the	at	I	party	→ _____	I was not at the party yesterday.
g)	Sue	cinema	at	the	last week	→ _____	Sue was not at the cinema last week.
h)	out	yesterday	They	→ _____	They were not out yesterday.

Simple Past – Short forms of (to) be – Negative forms: "wasn't" / "weren't"

a) Rewrite the sentences with the short forms of "be"!

Example:		
They were not friends.	→	They **weren't** friends.

a) I was not in Berlin.	**wasn't**	_____	I wasn't in Berlin.
b) I was not happy.		_____	I wasn't happy.
c) I was not late.		_____	I wasn't late.
d) She was not happy.	**wasn't**	_____	She wasn't happy.
e) He was not at the party.		_____	He wasn't at the party.
f) It was not warm.		_____	It wasn't warm.
g) We were not angry.	**weren't**	_____	We weren't angry.
h) You were not at home.		_____	You weren't at home.
i) They were not nice.		_____	They weren't nice.

b) Rewrite the sentences with the correct short form of "be"!

Example:			
She	was	not	here.
She	wasn't		here.
It	was	not	right.
			It wasn't right.
We	were	not	angry about it.
			We weren't angry about it.
That	was	not	fair.
			That wasn't fair.
He	was	not	at the party.
			He wasn't at the party.
They	were	not	on holiday.
			They weren't on holiday.
I	was	not	out.
			I wasn't out.
She	was	not	in my form.
			She wasn't in my form.
You	were	not	very happy.
			You weren't very happy.

Simple Past – Short forms of (to) be – Negative forms: "wasn't" / "weren't"

a) Rewrite the sentences and use the correct short form of "be"!

Example:
I <u>was not</u> sad.	→	I wasn't sad.
He <u>was not</u> my friend.	→	He wasn't my friend.
You <u>were not</u> happy.	→	You weren't happy.

Fold back!

a) My friends were not at home. → _____ My friends weren't …

b) We were not on holiday. → _____ We weren't on …

c) I was not angry. → _____ I wasn't angry.

d) It was not a big party. → _____ It wasn't a big party.

e) Peter was not in my form. → _____ Peter wasn't in my …

f) They were not happy about it. → _____ They weren't …

g) It was not interesting. → _____ It wasn't interesting.

h) They were not at the cinema. → _____ They weren't at …

i) She was not in Berlin. → _____ She wasn't in Berlin.

b) Form correct sentences!

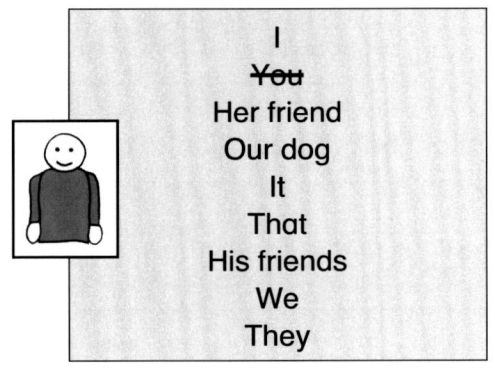

I
~~You~~
Her friend
Our dog
It
That
His friends
We
They

wasn't
weren't

at home.
~~at school.~~
at the cinema.
in the park.
a big party.
very interesting.
on holiday.
in Berlin.
at the disco.

Example: _____You_____ _____weren't_____ _____at school._____

1. _____
2. _____
3. _____
4. _____
5. _____
6. _____
7. _____
8. _____

Possible answers:
I wasn't at the cinema. / Her friend wasn't at home. / Our dog wasn't in the park. / It wasn't a big party. / That wasn't very interesting. / His friends weren't in Berlin. / We weren't at the disco. / They weren't on holiday.

Simple Past – Short forms of (to) be – Negative forms: "wasn't" / "weren't"

a) Fill in the correct negative short form of "be" in the Simple Past.

Example:
I _____ sad. → I <u>wasn't</u> sad.
He _____ my friend. → He <u>wasn't</u> my friend.
You _____ happy. → You <u>weren't</u> happy.

wasn't	a) That _____ a good idea.	j) I _____ angry at you.	wasn't
weren't	b) They _____ at the cinema.	k) My parents _____ on holiday.	weren't
wasn't	c) Mr Peters _____ my teacher.	l) Linda _____ in my team.	wasn't
weren't	d) We _____ in Hamburg.	m) It _____ my fault.	wasn't
wasn't	e) He _____ at the disco.	n) We _____ in the city.	weren't
weren't	f) You _____ at home.	o) Peter _____ at the market.	wasn't
weren't	g) Tom and Joe _____ friends.	p) Linda _____ late.	wasn't
weren't	h) The things _____ old.	q) Our friends _____ here.	weren't
wasn't	i) My room _____ dirty.	r) David _____ at school.	wasn't

b) Find the right order and add the correct negative short form of "be" ('m not / isn't / aren't).

Example: We { at { home. → We { weren't { at { home.

a) last month { I { in { Paris →		I wasn't in Paris last month.
b) at { They { angry { me →		They weren't angry at me.
c) idea { my { This →		This wasn't my idea.
d) yesterday { cinema { at { the { We →		We weren't at the cinema yesterday.
e) teacher { Mrs Smith { last year { my →		Mrs Smith wasn't my teacher last year.
f) many people { in { the { There { shop →		There weren't many people in the shop.
g) My { party { last { big →		My last party wasn't big.
h) I { at { home { alone →		I wasn't alone at home.

Simple Past – Questions with (to) be: "Was ...?" / "Were ...?"

Form questions!

Example:

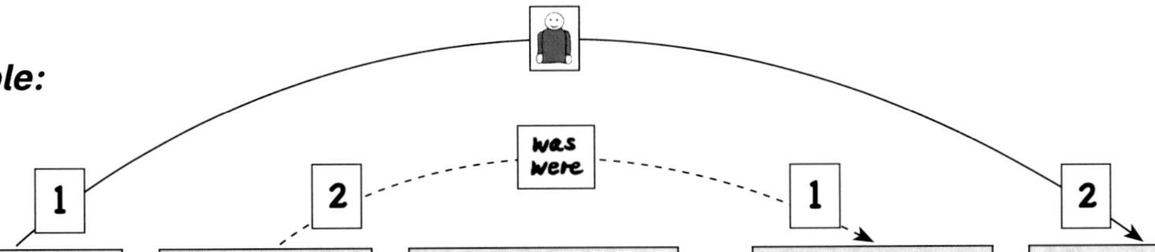

He	was	a friend.	→	Was	he	a friend?
They	were	new.		Were	they	new?

You	were	at home.	→			at home?
She	was	at the market.	→			at the market?
The Peters	were	on holiday.	→			on holiday?
You	were	angry.	→			angry?
Tom	was	here.	→			here?
They	were	happy.	→			happy?
It	was	sunny.	→			sunny?
Ina and Lu	were	at the party.	→			at the party?
He	was	a friend.	→			a friend?
You	were	in Berlin.	→			in Berlin?
The rooms	were	big.	→			big?
I	was	right.	→			right?
Linda	was	in her room.	→			in her room?
It	was	cold.	→			cold?

Answers:

Were you at home? Was Tom here?
Was she at the market? Were you angry?
Were the Peters on holiday? Was he a friend?
Were Ina and Lu at the party? Were you in Berlin?
Was it sunny? Was Linda in her room?
Were they happy? Was I right? Was it cold?
Were the rooms big?

Simple Past – Questions with (to) be: "Was …?" / "Were …?"

Form questions! Find the right order!

Example:

| He | was | a friend. | → | Was | he | a friend? |
| They | were | at home. | | Were | they | at home? |

1	2	was/were		Was/Were	1	2
was	that	my coke	→			
here	were	they	→			
it	funny	was	→			
were	these	your shoes	→			
it	was	your idea	→			
you	in Berlin	were	→			
Peter	was	at the shop	→			
were	at the party	Ina and Lu	→			
at the disco	your parents	were	→			
cold	was	it	→			
they	were	on a trip	→			
Sarah	in Paris	was	→			
were	you	angry	→			
the dog	in the garden	was	→			

Answers:

Was that my coke?
Were they here?
Was it funny?
Were these your shoes?
Was it your idea?
Were you in Berlin?
Was Peter at the shop?
Were Ina and Lu at the party?
Were your parents at the disco?
Was it cold?
Were they on a trip?
Was Sarah in Paris?
Were you angry?
Was the dog in the garden?

Turn over!

Simple Past – Questions with (to) be: "Was …?" / "Were …?"

a) Form questions!

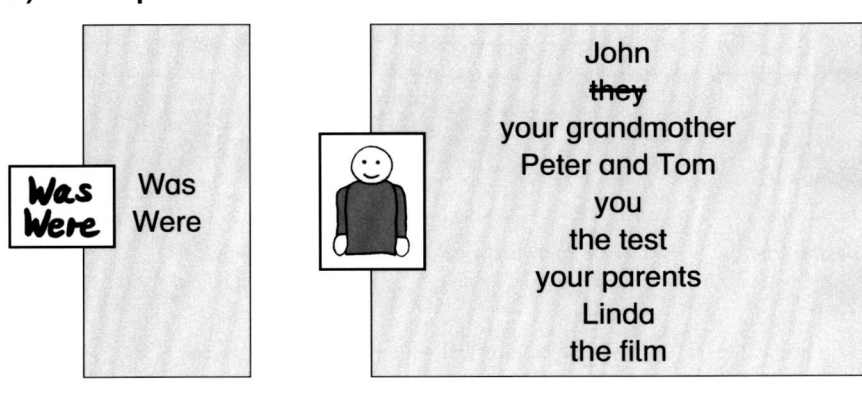

| Was / Were | John / ~~they~~ / your grandmother / Peter and Tom / you / the test / your parents / Linda / the film | late yesterday? / ~~in your class last year?~~ / a teacher? / at the party last night? / at home last weekend? / difficult? / in a restaurant last night? / with you at the cinema? / interesting? |

Example: Were — they — in your class last year?

1. _____
2. _____
3. _____
4. _____
5. _____
6. _____
7. _____
8. _____

Answers: Was John late yesterday? / Was your grandmother a teacher? / Were Peter and Tom at the party last night? / Were you at home last weekend? / Was the test difficult? / Were your parents in a restaurant last night? / Was Linda with you at the cinema? / Was the film interesting?

Turn over!

b) Find the right order for a question with "Was" / "Were"!

Example: We } were } late → Were } we } late?

Fold back!

a)	home } at } you } were	→	Were you at home?
b)	was } father } your } angry	→	Was your father angry?
c)	Tim and Joe } were } here	→	Were Tim and Joe here?
d)	sister } your } sad } was	→	Was your sister sad?
e)	it } your } idea } was	→	Was it your idea?
f)	Paris } in } were } you	→	Were you in Paris?

Simple Past – Short answers with (to) be: "was / wasn't" and "were / weren't"

a) Mark the right answer!

> Bei Kurzantworten übernimmst du oft die „be"-Form, mit der die Frage beginnt: **Was** he here? – Yes, he **was**. Bei Fragen, die direkt an dich gerichtet sind, antwortest du mit „I": **Were** you there? – Yes, I **was**.

Example:
Were you in London yesterday?   ○ Yes, I was.   ● No, I wasn't.

○	a) Tom <u>was</u> at the zoo yesterday.	○ Yes, he was.		i) It was rainy last week.	○ Yes, it was.	●
●	<u>Was</u> Tom at the cinema?	○ No, he wasn't.		Was it rainy last week?	○ No, it wasn't.	○
●	b) I <u>was</u> at home last night.	○ Yes, I was.		j) I was on holiday last year.	○ Yes, I was.	●
○	<u>Were</u> you at home last night?	○ No, I wasn't.		Were you on holiday last year?	○ No, I wasn't.	○
●	c) Our last party was cool.	○ Yes, it was.		k) They were in Berlin last week.	○ Yes, they were.	○
○	Was your last party cool?	○ No, it wasn't.		Were they in Bristol last week?	○ No, they weren't.	●
○	d) They were at home yesterday.	○ Yes, they were.		l) It was my idea.	○ Yes, it was.	●
●	Were they at the disco?	○ No, they weren't.		Was it your idea?	○ No, it wasn't.	○
○	e) It was cold last week.	○ Yes, it was.		m) Our dog Barker was in the park.	○ Yes, he was.	○
●	Was it hot last week?	○ No, it wasn't.		Was your dog in the garden?	○ No, he wasn't.	●
●	f) Sue was in my form last year. Was Sue in your form last year?	○ Yes, she was. ○ No, she wasn't.		n) Tina was ill yesterday. Was Tina ill yesterday?	○ Yes, she was. ○ No, she wasn't.	● ○
○	g) They were out last night.	○ Yes, they were.		o) We were at the disco last night.	○ Yes, we were.	○
●	Were they at home last night?	○ No, they weren't.		Were you at a restaurant?	○ No, we weren't.	●
●	h) I was late yesterday.	○ Yes, I was.		p) My dad was here an hour ago. Was your dad here an hour ago?	○ Yes, he was. ○ No, he wasn't.	● ○
○	Were you late yesterday?	○ No, I wasn't.				

b) Now you! Read the text and give short answers to the questions!

> Dear Linda!
> How are you? I am fine! How was your holiday in Italy? My holiday was great!
> We were in France. I was at the beach all the time. The weather was great.
> It was always sunny! We were in Paris too. It was very interesting.
> Love Sarah Miller

a)	<u>Was</u> Linda in Italy?	– Yes, she _____	Yes, she was.
b)	<u>Was</u> Sarah in Italy, too?	– No, she _____	No, she wasn't.
c)	<u>Were</u> the Millers in France?	– Yes, they _____	Yes, they were.
d)	<u>Was</u> Sarah in the city all the time?	– _____	No, she wasn't.
e)	<u>Was</u> the weather great?	– _____	Yes, it was.
f)	<u>Were</u> the Millers in Paris?	– _____	Yes, they were.
g)	<u>Was</u> Paris boring?	– _____	No, it wasn't.

Simple Past – Short answers with (to) be: "was / wasn't" and "were / weren't"

a) Form questions and short answers!

| Was | Tom your friend? | → | Yes, | he | was. |
| Were | they in Berlin? | | No, | they | weren't. |

| Was / Were | you 17 years old last year?
your friend in China last week?
it sunny yesterday?
your Maths teacher here an hour ago?
your friends in the park yesterday?
you and your friends on a school trip yesterday? | → | Yes,
No, | I
he / she / it
we
they | was
wasn't
were
weren't |

1. _____ → _____
2. _____ → _____
3. _____ → _____
4. _____ → _____
5. _____ → _____
6. _____ → _____

Answers:
1. Were you 17 … → Yes, I was. / No, I wasn't.
2. Was your friend in … → Yes, he / she was. / No, he / she wasn't.
3. Was it sunny … → Yes, it was. / No, it wasn't.
4. Was your Maths … → Yes, he / she was. / No, he / she wasn't.
5. Were your friends … → Yes, they were. / No, they weren't.
6. Were you and your … → Yes, we were. / No, we weren't.

Turn over!

b) Now you! Read the text and give short answers to the questions!

Hi Peter!
How are you? How was your holiday in Cardiff? And what was the weather like?
Here in Glasgow it was rainy. We were at the cinema, at a museum and also at a concert.
That was fun. We weren't at the beach. It was too cold.
Yours John Smith

Fold back!

a)	<u>Was</u> Peter in London?	– No, he _____	No, he wasn't.
b)	<u>Were</u> the Smiths in Glasgow?	– Yes, they _____	Yes, they were.
c)	<u>Was</u> John at the beach?	– No, _____	No, he wasn't.
d)	<u>Was</u> the weather fine?	– _____	No, it wasn't.
e)	<u>Were</u> the Smiths at the cinema?	– _____	Yes, they were.
f)	<u>Was</u> it cold?	– _____	Yes, it was.

Simple Past – Short answers with (to) be: "was / wasn't" and "were / weren't"

a) Form questions and short answers!

| Was | Tom your friend? | → | Yes, | he | was. |
| Were | they in Berlin? | → | No, | they | weren't. |

| Was / Were | you at home last weekend?
your best friend in Italy last week?
your German teacher here an hour ago?
it sunny yesterday?
your friends on a school trip last month?
you and your classmates at school yesterday? | → | Yes,
No, | ... | ... |

1. _____ → _____
2. _____ → _____
3. _____ → _____
4. _____ → _____
5. _____ → _____
6. _____ → _____

Answers:
1. Were you at home … → Yes, I was. / No, I wasn't.
2. Was your best friend … → Yes, he / she was. / No, he / she wasn't.
3. Was your German teacher … → Yes, he / she was. / No, he / she wasn't.
4. Was it sunny … → Yes, it was. / No, it wasn't.
5. Were your friends … → Yes, they were. / No, they weren't.
6. Were you and your … → Yes, we were. / No, we weren't.

Turn over!

b) Now you! Read the text and give short answers to the questions!

Hi Amy, hi Sue!
How are you? And how was your trip to Rome?
It was my birthday yesterday. Yesterday morning I was in the city centre
of London with my brother for an ice cream. The weather was great.
My birthday party was great, too. There were many friends at my party.
My father was there, too.
See you soon! Yours Dave

Fold back!

a) Were Amy and Sue in Rome?	–	_____	Yes, they were.
b) Was it Sue's birthday yesterday?	–	_____	No, it wasn't.
c) Was Dave in the centre with his brother?	–	_____	Yes, he was.
d) Were Dave's friends at the party?	–	_____	Yes, they were.
e) Was the party boring?	–	_____	No, it wasn't.
f) Was Dave's father at the party, too?	–	_____	Yes, he was.

Simple Past forms of (to) be – Activity: Tandem

Work with a partner. Fold the paper. One of you is partner A and the other is partner B. Partner A gives the answers for each gap. Partner B checks the answers. Then it's partner B's turn.

Simple Past forms of "be" (short forms): was / wasn't – were / weren't	Answers: Simple Past forms of "be"
Partner A	**Partner B**
a) +: I _____ at home yesterday.	a) I _was_ at home yesterday.
b) –: He _____ in Berlin last week.	b) He _wasn't_ in Berlin last week.
c) +: They _____ on a trip last month.	c) They _were_ on a trip last month.
d) –: Linda _____ angry at you.	d) Linda _wasn't_ angry at you.
e) +: We _____ in Year 5 last year.	e) We _were_ in Year 5 last year.
f) +: It _____ warm yesterday.	f) It _was_ warm yesterday.
g) –: He _____ my teacher last year.	g) He _wasn't_ my teacher last year.
h) +: You _____ late yesterday.	h) You _were_ late yesterday.
i) +: Peter and Lynn _____ here a minute ago.	i) Peter and Lynn _were_ here a minute ago.
j) –: Your friends _____ in Paris last month.	j) Your friends _weren't_ in Paris last month.
k) +: I _____ at a party last night.	k) I _was_ at a party last night.

Answers: Simple Past forms of "be"	Simple Past forms of "be" (short forms): was / wasn't – were / weren't
Partner A	**Partner B**
a) Tom _was_ in my class last year.	a) +: Tom _____ in my class last year.
b) We _weren't_ in Berlin last year.	b) –: We _____ in Berlin last year.
c) My friends _were_ angry at me.	c) +: My friends _____ angry at me.
d) I _wasn't_ on the school trip yesterday.	d) –: I _____ on the school trip yesterday.
e) It _was_ very cold last week.	e) +: It _____ very cold last week.
f) She _was_ in my football team last year.	f) +: She _____ in my football team last year.
g) They _weren't_ in my form.	g) –: They _____ in my form.
h) Mrs Miller _was_ my teacher last year.	h) +: Mrs Miller _____ my teacher last year.
i) Peter _was_ in Scotland a month ago.	i) +: Peter _____ in Scotland a month ago.
j) Your friends _weren't_ at the disco last night.	j) –: Your friends _____ at the disco last night.
k) You _were_ too late.	k) +: You _____ too late.

Simple Past – Questions with (to) be: question word + "was" / "were"

Sort the parts and form questions!

Example:

| Where | your friend | was | → | Where | was | your friend? |
| these | were | Whose shoes | → | Whose shoes | were | these? |

				?	was/were	
was	Tom's party	When	→			Tom's party?
Where	were	your books	→			your books?
What	the weather like	was	→			the weather like?
was	at the disco	Who	→			at the disco?
When	his birthday	was	→			his birthday?
they	Where	were	→			they?
he at home	was	Why	→			he at home?
was	Whose party	it	→			it?
it	How much	was	→			it?
How many people	there	were	→			there?
the concert	was	When	→			the concert?
Whose idea	it	was	→			it?
were	Which films	good	→			good?

Answers:
1. When was Tom's party?
2. Where were your books?
3. What was the weather like?
4. Who was at the disco?
5. When was his birthday?
6. Where were they?
7. Why was he at home?
8. Whose party was it?
9. How much was it?
10. How many people were there?
11. When was the concert?
12. Whose idea was it?
13. Which films were good?

Turn over!

Simple Past – Questions with (to) be: question word + "was" / "were"

Sort the parts and form questions!

Example:

Where	your friend	was	→	Where	was	your friend?
her cats	were	Where		Where	were	her cats?

				?	was / were	
was	When	your birthday	→			
Where	your bag	was	→			
they	were	Where	→			
was	it	Which room	→			
Whose idea	was	it	→			
your friends	were	Who	→			
was	the test	When	→			
How far	the trip	was	→			
was	she at home	Why	→			
were	How often	you there	→			
his pens	were	Where	→			
How much	it	was	→			
your hair	How long	was	→			

Answers:

1. When was your birthday?
2. Where was your bag?
3. Where were they?
4. Which room was it?
5. Whose idea was it?
6. Who were your friends?
7. When was the test?
8. How far was the trip?
9. Why was she at home?
10. How often were you there?
11. Where were his pens?
12. How much was it?
13. How long was your hair?

Turn over!

Simple Past – Questions with (to) be: question word + "was" / "were"

Form questions!

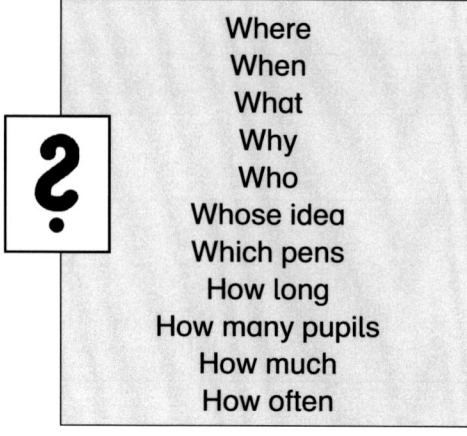

Where		your shirts?
When		the concert?
What		the weather like?
Why	was	Tom at home?
Who	were	at the party?
Whose idea		it?
Which pens		in the bag?
How long		the school trip?
How many pupils		at the school disco?
How much		the CDs?
How often		you there?

Example: _Where_ _was_ _your friend?_

1. ___
2. ___
3. ___
4. ___
5. ___
6. ___
7. ___
8. ___
9. ___
10. ___
11. ___

Answers:

1. Where were your shirts?
2. When was the concert?
3. What was the weather like?
4. Why was Tom at home?
5. Who was at the party?
6. Whose idea was it?
7. Which pens were in the bag?
8. How long was the school trip?
9. How many pupils were at the school disco?
10. How much were the CDs?
11. How often were you there?

Turn over!

Simple Past – Positive statements with regular verbs ("verb-ed")

Form positive statements! Say what these people did.

Example: Yesterday we ___ together.	○ looked ○ worked ● played		
a) I ___ at home yesterday.	○ painted (1a) ○ helped (2a) ○ stayed (3a)	e) They ___ the old man.	○ helped (1e) ○ walked (2e) ○ worked (3e)
b) Peter and Tim ___ football.	○ played (1b) ○ invited (2b) ○ arrived (3b)	f) My friends ___ TV.	○ painted (1f) ○ stayed (2f) ○ watched (3f)
c) You ___ the door yesterday.	○ walked (1c) ○ painted (2c) ○ looked (3c)	g) I ___ my friend last week.	○ phoned (1g) ○ played (2g) ○ started (3g)
d) We ___ at the bus stop.	○ painted (1d) ○ stopped (2d) ○ waited (3d)	h) They ___ to her an hour ago.	○ helped (1h) ○ talked (2h) ○ waited (3h)

Answers: 3a – 1b – 2c – 3d – 1e – 3f – 1g – 2h

Turn over!

Simple Past – Positive statements with regular verbs ("verb-ed")

Say what these people did. Fill in the gaps and use the Simple Past of the verbs in the verb box.

Example: We ___ together. → We <u>waited</u> together.

Fold back!	watch – laugh – play – visit – help – listen		talk – walk – dance – pack – stop – wait	Fold back!
played	a) I ___ football yesterday.	g) The car ___ behind the van.	stopped
watched	b) Peter and Tim ___ TV.	h) I ___ to her on the phone.	talked
listened	c) You ___ to your new CD.	i) She ___ at the bus stop.	waited
helped	d) He ___ Tina with her homework.	j) They ___ a lot at the disco.	danced
laughed	e) The girls ___ at his jokes.	k) The boys ___ to school.	walked
visited	f) They ___ a museum.	l) We ___ our bags.	packed

Simple Past – Positive statements with regular verbs ("verb-ed")

Form positive statements! Say what these people did.

Example: We <u>listened</u> to him.

danced	a) I _____.		e) I _____ dinner.	cooked
played	b) Peter and Tim _____ football.		f) She _____ him.	stopped
opened	c) You _____ the door.		g) They _____ a lot.	laughed
washed	d) He _____ his hands.		h) He _____ the room.	cleaned

Simple Past – Positive statements with irregular verbs

Form positive statements! Say what these people did.

Example: He _____ a letter.   ○ went   ● wrote

●○	a) They ____ their homework.	○ did ○ made	f) My brother ____ a coke.	○ ate ○ drank	○●
○●	b) Peter ____ a new CD.	○ rode ○ bought	g) My friends ____ a party.	○ had ○ were	●○
○●	c) My friend ____ to the cinema.	○ said ○ went	h) We ____ our bikes.	○ rode ○ wrote	●○
●○	d) I ____ her a flower.	○ gave ○ ate	i) My sister ____ a bike.	○ became ○ got	○●
○●	e) She ____ a funny book.	○ rode ○ read	j) We ____ her at school.	○ saw ○ went	●○

Simple Past – Positive statements with irregular verbs

Say what these people did. Fill in the gaps and use the Simple Past of the verbs in the verb box.

	Example: We _____ together. → We ran together.		
Fold back!	see – do – buy – go – read – be	ride – write – get – have – give – take	Fold back!
read	a) I _____ a book yesterday.	g) Tom _____ me his book.	gave
went	b) Peter and Tim _____ to school by bus.	h) I _____ a bike last year.	got
were	c) You _____ at home yesterday.	i) She _____ her bike to school.	rode
did	d) He _____ his homework.	j) They _____ the bus home.	took
saw	e) The girls _____ Tom at school.	k) The boys _____ a big party.	had
bought	f) They _____ a new CD.	l) We _____ our mother a postcard.	wrote

---

Simple Past – Positive statements with irregular verbs

Form positive statements! Say what these people did.

	Example: I heard him.		
Fold back!			Fold back!
read	a) I _____ a nice book last week.	e) I _____ the whole day.	slept
did	b) They _____ their homework.	f) Tom _____ out his books.	took
gave	c) Tina _____ John her hand.	g) They _____ a race.	ran
rode	d) He _____ his bike yesterday.	h) He _____ a letter to his mum.	wrote

Simple Past – Spelling – Activity: Sorting

Write down the verbs in the correct spelling box!

consonant after **a short, stressed vowel** at the end of the verb: **Double it!**

I st<u>o</u>p. → I stopped.

verbs ending with **consonant + -y:** *Change y to i + -ed!*

I c<u>r</u>y. → I tried.

hurry – swap – live – carry – cancel – copy – study – close – phone – try – level – plan – prefer – smile – agree – rub

verbs ending with **-e:** *Add only -d!*

I lov<u>e</u>. → I loved.

In British English, **-l at the end:** *Double it!*

I trave<u>l</u>. → I travelled.

Answers:

1: swapped – planned – preferred – rubbed
2: lived – closed – phoned – smiled – agreed
3: cancelled – levelled
4: hurried – carried – copied – studied – tried

 Turn over!

Simple Past and adverbs of frequency – Activity: Cutting out

Die Signalwörter „yesterday", „last", „ago", „in ..." können zu Beginn oder am Ende des Satzes stehen.

Cut out the word boxes and put the parts into the correct order.

Example:

| Yesterday | I | invited | Tina | for dinner. |
| I | invited | Tina | for dinner | yesterday. |

played (1a)	they (1b)	tennis (1c)	at the club (1d)	last week (1e)
in 2013 (2a)	my mother (2b)	moved (2c)	to Paris (2d)	in France (2e)
he (3a)	a month ago (3b)	in Munich (3c)	went (3d)	to a museum (3e)
last Monday (4a)	I (4b)	saw (4c)	at the bus stop (4d)	Lynn and Sue (4e)
bought (5a)	Mr Smith (5b)	a year ago (5c)	his wife (5d)	a car (5e)
for dinner (6a)	a pizza (6b)	had (6c)	yesterday (6d)	Tom (6e)
in Australia (7a)	in 2011 (7b)	they (7c)	flew (7d)	to Sydney (7e)
yesterday (8a)	wrote (8b)	I (8c)	her (8d)	a letter (8e)
Linda (9a)	months ago (9b)	at the mall (9c)	bought (9d)	Sue's present (9e)
had (10a)	last year (10b)	we (10c)	a big party (10d)	at the pool (10e)
in 2000 (11a)	enjoyed (11b)	the firework (11c)	everybody (11d)	outside (11e)
a good film (12a)	was (12b)	yesterday (12c)	on TV (12d)	there (12e)

Answers:
1e-1b-1c-1d-(1e) / 2a-2b-2c-2d-2e-(2a) / 3b-3a-3d-3e-3c-(3b) / 4a-4b-4c-4e-4d-(4a) /
5c-5b-5a-5d-5e-(5c) / 6d-6e-6c-6b-6a-(6d) / 7b-7c-7d-7e-7a-(7b) / 8a-8c-8b-8d-8e-(8a) /
9b-9a-9d-9e-9c-(9b) / 10b-10c-10a-10d-10e-(10b) / 11a-11d-11b-11c-11e-(11a) /
12c-12e-12b-12a-12d-(12c)

 Turn over!

Simple Past – Negative statements with "didn't"

Form negative statements!

> Für die Verneinung im Simple Past gilt:
> **didn't + infinitive**

Example:
I bought a present. → I _didn't buy_ a present.

a) She helped her dad. →	She		her dad.	She didn't help her dad.
b) We played football. →	We		football.	We didn't play football.
c) He walked home. →				He didn't walk home.
d) I listened to the CD. →				I didn't listen to the CD.
e) They worked here. →				They didn't work here.
f) My friend called me. →				My friend didn't call me.
g) I cleaned my room. →				I didn't clean my room.
h) They wrote a story. →				They didn't write a story.
i) My sisters went home. →				My sisters didn't go home.

Simple Past – Negative statements with "didn't"

Form negative statements!

> Für die Verneinung im Simple Past gilt:
> **didn't + infinitive**

Example:
I bought a present. → I _didn't buy_ a present.

a) We bought a new CD. →			We didn't buy a new CD.
b) We took photos. →			We didn't take photos.
c) He ran home. →			He didn't run home.
d) I rode my bike. →			I didn't ride my bike.
e) They wrote a letter to her. →			They didn't write a letter to her.
f) My friend got a bike. →			My friend didn't get a bike.
g) Tina saw him at school. →			Tina didn't see him at school.
h) They had a big party. →			They didn't have a big party.
i) My sisters went home. →			My sisters didn't go home.

Simple Past – Negative statements with "didn't"

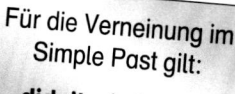

Form positive and negative statements!
Say what these people did and what they didn't do yesterday.

Für die Verneinung im Simple Past gilt:
didn't + infinitive

Example: I <u>bought</u> a book but I <u>didn't buy</u> a CD yesterday.
We <u>repaired</u> the bike but we <u>didn't repair</u> the car last week.

1. paint: I _____ my room but I _____ _____ the kitchen.   *painted – didn't paint*
2. watch: We _____ a film but we _____ _____ a game show.   *watched – didn't watch*
3. play: You _____ the piano but you _____ _____ the drums.   *played – didn't play*
4. read: I _____ comics but I _____ _____ books.   *read – didn't read*
5. eat: They _____ tomatoes but they _____ _____ carrots.   *ate – didn't eat*
6. go: I _____ swimming but I _____ _____ shopping.   *went – didn't go*
7. see: We _____ Tom at school but we _____ _____ Sarah.   *saw – didn't see*
8. get: My mother _____ a bike but she _____ _____ a car.   *got – didn't get*
9. drink: I _____ tea but I _____ _____ coffee.   *drank – didn't drink*

Fold back!

Simple Past – Questions with "did"

Questions: did + person + infinitive

Form questions! Find the correct verb for each question!

1. Did you	rain	for our drinks last night?
2. Did Tom	do	a letter to their grandmother?
3. Did your mother	win	all the milk yesterday?
4. Did it	drink	your homework yesterday?
5. Did the cat	pay	the football match?
6. Did your football team	eat	her friend at a café last week?
7. Did we	meet	the whole day?
8. Did they	write	his sandwich for lunch?

Example: <u>Did you</u> <u>play</u> <u>tennis yesterday?</u>

1. _____
2. _____
3. _____
4. _____
5. _____
6. _____
7. _____
8. _____

Answers:
1. Did you do your homework yesterday?
2. Did Tom eat his sandwich for lunch?
3. Did your mother meet her friend at a café last week?
4. Did it rain the whole day?
5. Did the cat drink all the milk yesterday?
6. Did your football team win the football match?
7. Did we pay for our drinks last night?
8. Did they write a letter to their grandmother?

Turn over!

Simple Past – Questions with "did"

Form questions!

> **Questions:** did + person + infinitive

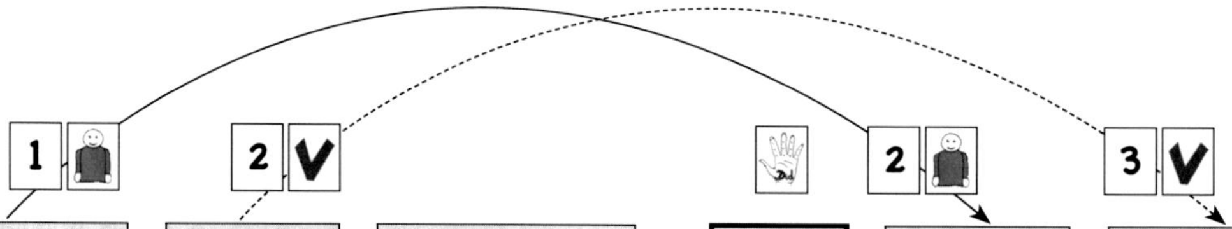

1	2 ✓			2	3 ✓	
They	sang	a song.	Did	they	sing	a song?
He	worked	a lot.	Did	he	work	a lot?
Bill and Joe	cleaned	their rooms. →				their rooms?
Tom	stayed	at home. →				at home?
Mr Miller	talked	to us. →				to us?
They	listened	to the CD. →				to the CD?
Joe and Sue	walked	to school. →				to school?
It	rained	a lot. →				a lot?
The Millers	went	on holiday. →				on holiday?
You	ate	my sandwich. →				my sandwich?
They	came	home early. →				home early?
Bill	bought	a present. →				a present?
The pupils	did	their homework. →				their homework?
Sarah	wrote	a postcard. →				a postcard?

Answers:
1. Did Bill and Joe clean …?
2. Did Tom stay …?
3. Did Mr Miller talk …?
4. Did they listen …?
5. Did Joe and Sue walk …?
6. Did it rain …?
7. Did the Millers go …?
8. Did you eat …?
9. Did they come …?
10. Did Bill buy …?
11. Did the pupils do …?
12. Did Sarah write …?

Turn over!

Simple Past – Questions with "did"

Form questions!

Questions: did + person + infinitive

They	sang	a song.	→ Did	they	sing	a song?
He	worked	a lot.	→ Did	he	work	a lot?
Her sister	played	the piano.	→			
Our rooms	looked	dirty.	→			
His teacher	helped	him.	→			
My friend	cleaned	his room.	→			
It	rained	a lot.	→			
Linda	wrote	a letter.	→			
The dog	slept	in the basket.	→			
Tom	bought	a book.	→			
They	ate	lunch.	→			
The girls	ran	around.	→			
He	did	his homework.	→			
They	went	on holiday.	→			
Tim and Jo	rode	their bikes.	→			
The cat	drank	the milk.	→			

Answers:

1. Did her sister play the piano?
2. Did our rooms look dirty?
3. Did his teacher help him?
4. Did my friend clean his room?
5. Did it rain a lot?
6. Did Linda write a letter?
7. Did the dog sleep in the basket?
8. Did Tom buy a book?
9. Did they eat lunch?
10. Did the girls run around?
11. Did he do his homework?
12. Did they go on holiday?
13. Did Tim and Jo ride their bikes?
14. Did the cat drink the milk?

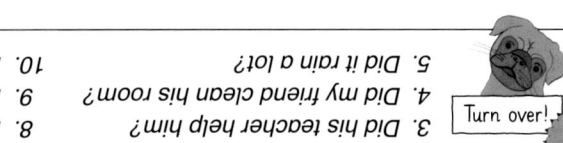

Simple Past – Questions and short answers with "did"

Look at each statement and the question. Mark the correct short answer for each question.

Example:
Did you see him yesterday?
○ Yes, I did
● No, I didn't.

●	a) Lynn went on holiday last Friday. Did Lynn go on holiday last Friday?	○ Yes, she did. ○ No, she didn't.	g) He won the last race. Did he win the last race?	○ Yes, he did. ○ No, he didn't.	● ○
○ ●	b) They walked to school yesterday. Did they ride to school by bike?	○ Yes, they did. ○ No, they didn't.	h) I ate a pizza for lunch. Did you eat a soup?	○ Yes, I did. ○ No, I didn't.	○ ●
○ ●	c) Last year he bought a house. Did he buy a car last year?	○ Yes, he did. ○ No, he didn't.	i) Sue called Tim. Did Sue call John?	○ Yes, she did. ○ No, she didn't.	○ ●
● ○	d) It rained a lot last week. Did it rain a lot?	○ Yes, it did. ○ No, it didn't.	j) Mr Smith bought a book. Did he buy a flower?	○ Yes, he did. ○ No, he didn't.	○ ●
● ○	e) My friends went to the party. Did your friends go to the party?	○ Yes, they did. ○ No, they didn't.	k) I wrote my mum a letter. Did you write to your dad?	○ Yes, I did. ○ No, I didn't.	○ ●
● ○	f) Mr Smith talked to her last week. Did he talk to her last week?	○ Yes, he did. ○ No, he didn't.	l) They moved to Berlin. Did they move to Paris?	○ Yes, they did. ○ No, they didn't.	○ ●

Simple Past – Questions and short answers with "did"

Form questions and short answers!

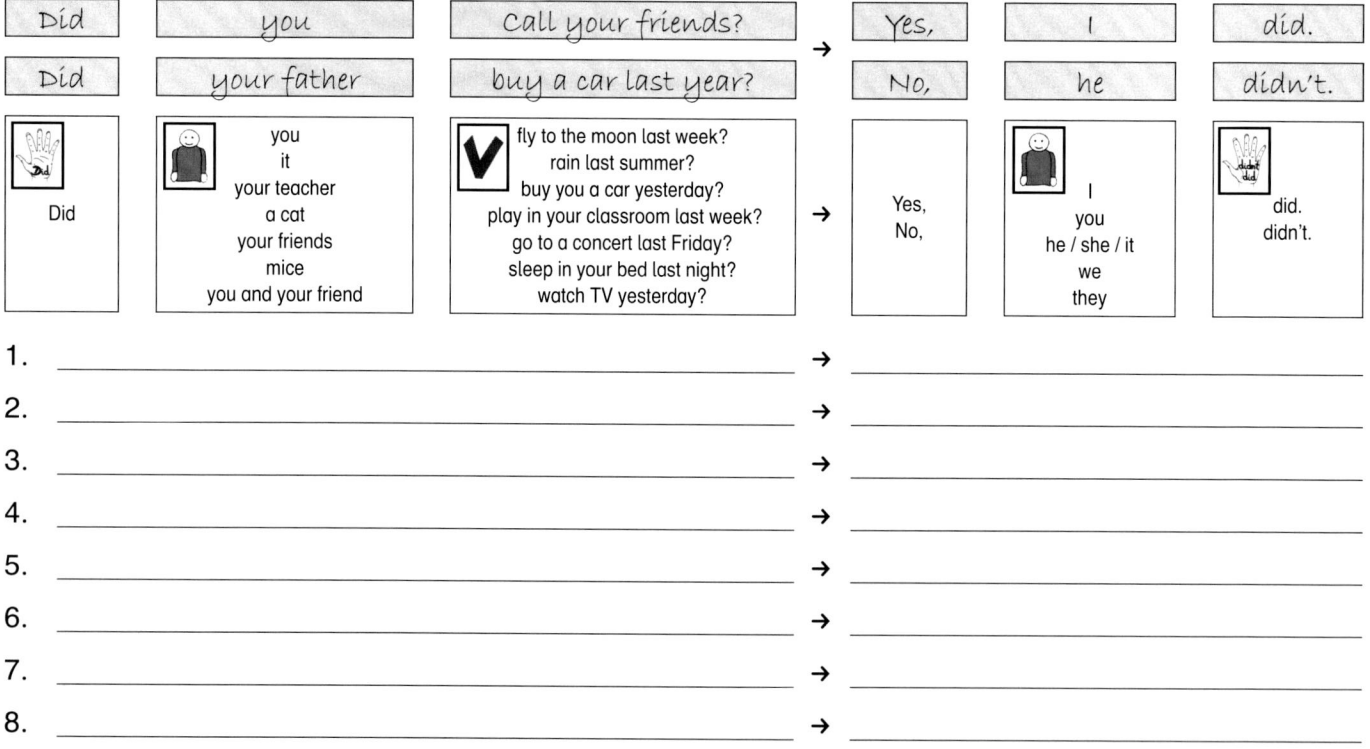

1. _____ → _____
2. _____ → _____
3. _____ → _____
4. _____ → _____
5. _____ → _____
6. _____ → _____
7. _____ → _____
8. _____ → _____

Answers:
Did you fly to the moon last week? – No, I didn't.
Did it rain last summer? – Yes, it did.
Did your teacher buy you a car yesterday? – No, he / she didn't.
Did a cat play in your classroom last week? – No, it didn't.
Did your friends go to a concert last Friday? – Yes, they did. / No, they didn't.
Did mice sleep in your bed last night? – No, they didn't.
Did you and your friends watch TV yesterday? – Yes, we did. / No, we didn't.

Simple Past – Questions and short answers with "did"

Form questions and short answers! Match the correct parts from each box!

| Did | you | Call your friends? | → | Yes, | I | did. |
| Did | your father | buy a car last year? | | No, | he | didn't. |

| Did | you / a friend / your teacher / it / a cat / your friends / you and your friend / elephants | ✓ go to school yesterday? / do your homework last week? / buy you a dog a week ago? / snow last summer? / teach you Maths yesterday? / paint your room last night? / watch TV yesterday? / play in your bedroom last week? | → | Yes, No, | ... | ... |

1. _____ → _____

2. _____ → _____

3. _____ → _____

4. _____ → _____

5. _____ → _____

6. _____ → _____

7. _____ → _____

8. _____ → _____

Answers:
1. Did you go to school yesterday? – Yes, I did. / No, I didn't.
2. Did a friend do your homework last week? – Yes, he / she did. / No, he / she didn't.
3. Did your teacher buy you a dog a week ago? – No, he / she didn't.
4. Did it snow last summer? – No, it didn't.
5. Did a cat teach you Maths yesterday? – No, it didn't.
6. Did your friends paint your room last night? – No, they didn't.
7. Did you and your friend watch TV yesterday? – Yes, we did. / No, we didn't.
8. Did elephants play in your bedroom last week? – No, they didn't.

Turn over!

Simple Past – Questions with question words

Form questions! Find the correct order!

Example:

| did | you | Where | go? | → | Where | did | you | go? |
| he | When | did | get up? | → | When | did | he | get up? |

buy?	Which pen	you	did	→			you	buy?
did	How long	wait?	he	→			he	wait?
do?	did	they	What	→			they	do?
Sarah	Whose hat	did	lose?	→			Sarah	lose?
When	did	end?	the match	→				
it	How much	cost?	did	→				
Why	you	laugh?	did	→				
did	she	Where	go?	→				
did	How often	meet?	you	→				
Why	did	Linda	cry?	→				
did	move?	When	they	→				
did	Which shirt	you	buy?	→				
What	do?	did	he	→				
see?	you	did	Who	→				

Answers:

Which pen did you buy? / How long did he wait? / What did they do? / Whose hat did Sarah lose? / When did the match end? / How much did it cost? / Why did you laugh? / Where did she go? / How often did you meet? / Why did Linda cry? / When did they move? / Which shirt did you buy? / What did he do? / Who did you see?

Turn over!

Simple Past – Questions with question words

Form questions with question words!

?	did		
What	did	Peter and Tom go yesterday?	Peter and Tom went to the zoo.
Where		the CD cost?	The CD cost £7.
When		Jenny travel last year?	She travelled far, about 2000 miles.
Why		the boys come home last night?	The boys came home at 3 o'clock.
Who		Bill stay at home last Friday?	Because Bill was ill.
Whose bike		your mother buy at the shop?	My mother bought a new shirt.
Which colour		you call yesterday morning?	I called the doctor.
How long		Tom water the flowers last week?	Tom watered the flowers 2 times.
How much		the Millers stay in Italy last month?	The Millers stayed 2 weeks.
How often		your father choose for your room?	My father chose yellow.
How far		Jim repair last weekend?	Jim repaired my bike.

Schau auf die Antworten. Diese helfen dir, das richtige Fragewort zu finden.

Example: Where did you play tennis?

1. _____
2. _____
3. _____
4. _____
5. _____
6. _____
7. _____
8. _____
9. _____
10. _____
11. _____

Answers:
1. What did your mother buy at the shop? – My mother bought a new shirt.
2. Where did Peter and Tom go yesterday? – Peter and Tom went to the zoo.
3. When did the boys come home last night? – The boys came home at 3 o'clock.
4. Why did Bill stay at home last Friday? – Because Bill was ill.
5. Who did you call yesterday morning? – I called the doctor.
6. Whose bike did Jim repair last weekend? – Jim repaired my bike.
7. Which colour did your father choose for your room? – My father chose yellow.
8. How long did the Millers stay in Italy last month? – The Millers stayed 2 weeks.
9. How much did the CD cost? – The CD cost £7.
10. How often did Tom water the flowers last week? – Tom watered the flowers 2 times.
11. How far did Jenny travel last year? – She travelled far, about 2000 miles.

 Turn over!

Simple Past – Questions with question words

Ask for the underlined parts.

Example: I ate an apple yesterday.

What	did	you	eat	yesterday?

1. They met Tim <u>at 7 o'clock last Friday</u>.

2. I played <u>football</u> last Wednesday.

3. Linda stayed at home last week <u>because she was ill</u>.

4. Last week the shirt cost <u>£5</u> at the supermarket.

5. We walked <u>20 minutes</u> to school yesterday.

6. My father worked <u>in Munich</u> in last year.

7. I repaired <u>my sister's</u> bike yesterday evening.

8. He visited the <u>art</u> museum yesterday.

Answers:

1. When did they meet Tim?
2. What did you play last Wednesday? (You don't ask yourself: "What did I play?")
3. Why did Linda stay at home last week?
4. What did the shirt cost at the supermarket last week?
5. How long did you / we walk to school yesterday?
6. Where did your father work last year?
7. Whose bike did you repair yesterday evening?
8. Which museum did he visit yesterday?

Turn over!

Simple Past – Questions ending with a preposition

a) Look at the statement and the question. Mark the right preposition for each question.

Example: Who did you sing _____?
○ to
○ in
● for

I sang **for** my friends yesterday.

a) Last year I worked <u>at a fashion shop</u>.
Where did you work _____?
○ in (o)
○ with (c)
○ at (e)

b) Last week my teacher talked <u>to my mum</u>.
Who did your teacher talk __?
○ to (x)
○ for (j)
○ with (t)

c) I gave the present <u>to Jenny</u>.
Who did you give it _____?
○ at (p)
○ to (c)
○ in (o)

d) Yesterday we played <u>with our dog</u>.
Who did you play _____?
○ from (j)
○ with (e)
○ for (b)

e) Last year he was interested <u>in a new car</u>.
What was he interested _____?
○ for (e)
○ at (b)
○ in (l)

f) The last film I saw was <u>about an old man</u>.
What was the last film _____?
○ about (l)
○ with (b)
○ for (x)

g) Yesterday I spoke <u>to Linda</u>.
Who did you speak _____?
○ to (e)
○ of (j)
○ in (o)

h) The presents were <u>for my mum</u>.
Who were the presents _____?
○ of (b)
○ in (e)
○ for (n)

i) She went on holiday <u>with Tim</u>.
Who did she go on holiday _____?
○ for (x)
○ with (t)
○ in (c)

j) He bought the tickets <u>for her</u>.
Who did he buy the tickets _____?
○ about (b)
○ for (j)
○ of (e)

k) Last week I made tea <u>for friends</u>.
Who did you make tea _____?
○ on (c)
○ with (t)
○ for (o)

l) We listened <u>to the CD</u> an hour ago.
What did you listen _____?
○ about (x)
○ from (e)
○ to (b)

Write down the letter behind each answer. Keep to the order a, b, c ...
If your answers are correct you can read your code:

__ __ __ __ __ __ __   __ __ __!

b) Now you! Fill in a correct preposition (to / at / for ...)!

a) Who did you talk _____ yesterday?

b) What were you interested _____?

c) Who did he wait _____?

d) Where did the old man come _____?

e) Who did you listen _____?

f) Who did she play _____?

Fold back!

to

in

for

from

to

with

Simple Past – Questions ending with a preposition

Example: *I sang **for my friends** yesterday.*

Who   did   you   sing _____?

○ to
○ in
● for

Fill in the correct preposition from the preposition box!

for	to
with	at
about	to
to	with
about	on
for	to
for	to
about	from
in	to

1. "Who did you give my number _____?" – "I gave it to a friend."
2. "What did you put the sweets _____?" – "I put them in a small box."
3. "What did he work _____ last year?" – "He worked on a history book."
4. "Who did you have lunch _____?" – "I had lunch with my friend Peter."
5. "Which university did you go _____?" – "I went to CMU."
6. "Who did you play football _____?" – "I played with Tim and Peter."
7. "Who did you send the letter _____?" – "I sent it to Linda."
8. "Who did you do the painting _____?" – "I did the painting for my mum."
9. "What did you talk _____?" – "We talked about the school trip."
10. "Which CD did you listen _____?" – "I listened to a Christmas CD."
11. "What did you need that picture _____?" – "I needed it for my homework."
12. "Who did you talk _____ a minute ago?" – "I talked to Peter."
13. "Which concert did you go _____ last night?" – "I went to a pop concert."
14. "What was the film _____?" – "The film was about dinosaurs."
15. "Who did you buy the book _____?" – "I bought the book from Jenny."
16. "Who did you make these muffins _____?" – "I made these muffins for my party guests."
17. "What was your dream _____?" – "My dream was about a lonely island."
18. "Which hotel did they stay _____?" – "They stayed at the Holiday Inn."

Answers: 1. to 2. in 3. on 4. with 5. to 6. with 7. to 8. for 9. about 10. to 11. for 12. to 13. to 14. about 15. from 16. for 17. about 18. at

Turn over!

Simple Past – Questions ending with a preposition

Ask for the underlined parts.

Example:		I	sang	for my friends.
Who	did	you	sing	for?
1. Yesterday I talked <u>to my grandparents</u>.			
2. We made the cake <u>for Sarah</u>.			
3. He bought the car <u>from a friend</u>.			
4. Last Friday we played football <u>with our friends</u>.			
5. Yesterday morning Tom waited <u>for his friend</u>.			
6. Last week my teacher spoke <u>to my parents</u>.			
7. Yesterday evening my boyfriend paid <u>for me</u>.			
8. My friend worked <u>on his project</u> last night.			

Answers:
1. Who did you talk to yesterday?
2. Who did you make the cake for?
3. Who did he buy the car from?
4. Who did you play football with?
5. Who did Tom wait for yesterday morning?
6. Who did your teacher speak to?
7. Who did your boyfriend pay for?
8. What did your friend work on last night?

Turn over!

Possessive pronouns

I → mine	we → ours
you → yours	you → yours
he → his	they → theirs
she → hers	
it → its	

Mark the right answer!

Example: This is <u>my pen</u>. → It is ___.
- ○ hers
- ● mine
- ○ its

a) This is <u>my book</u>. →	It is ___.	○ mine ○ it ○ them	● ○ ○
b) This is <u>Tina's school bag</u>. →	It is ___.	○ his ○ hers ○ its	○ ● ○
c) These are the <u>children's balls</u>. →	They are ___.	○ theirs ○ ours ○ its	● ○ ○
d) This is <u>Peter and my room</u>. →	It is ___.	○ mine ○ his ○ ours	○ ○ ●
e) These are <u>Peter's books</u>. →	They are ___.	○ hers ○ his ○ theirs	○ ● ○
f) This is <u>your sandwich</u>. →	It is ___.	○ mine ○ hers ○ yours	○ ○ ●
g) These are <u>Sue and Tim's pens</u>. →	They are ___.	○ hers ○ his ○ theirs	○ ○ ●

Possessive pronouns

Fill in the correct possessive pronoun (mine / yours /…)!

Example: Tim: "Is this my bag?" – Sue: "Yes, that bag is <u>yours</u>!"

yours	a) Lisa: "Is that my apple?" Tom: "Yes, it's _____!"	f) John: "Is this Sue and Lynn's room?" Tim: "Yes, it's _____."	theirs
ours	b) Till and Joe: "Where are our bikes?" Till: "Ah, look! There are _____!"	g) Ronda: "Is this my sandwich?" Joe: "Yes, it's _____."	yours
his	c) Ben: "Is this Sam's book?" Lisa: "Yes, it's _____."	h) Ed: "Are these our bags?" Joe: "Yes, they are _____."	ours
mine	d) Joe: "Is this your chair, Lynn?" Lynn: "Yes, it's _____."	i) Sarah: "Is this your picture, Tom?" Tom: "Yes, it's _____."	mine
hers	e) Tom: "Is this Linda's ball?" Laura: "Yes, it's _____."	j) Joe: "Where is my pencil case?" Sue: "Here is _____."	yours

46 Freiarbeitsmaterialien für die 6. Klasse: Englisch

Possessive pronouns

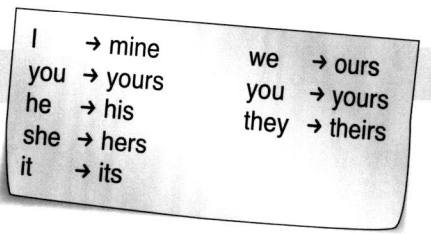

Possessive determiner (my / your / his / ...)
or possessive pronoun (mine / yours / ...)?
Mark the right answer!

	Example: Tim: "Where is <u>my</u> bag?"	● my ○ his ○ her	Sue: "Here is <u>yours</u>!"	● yours ○ your ○ my	
● ○ ○	a) Lisa: "This is Peter. He is ___ friend."	○ my ○ his ○ hers	f) Tom: "Where are my keys?" Sue: "Here are ___!"	○ yours ○ your ○ my	● ○ ○
○ ● ○	b) Tom: "Is this Tina's shoe?" Sue: "Yes, it's ___."	○ mine ○ hers ○ her	g) Ben: "Is this Peter's bag?" Jill: "No, that is not ___ bag."	○ my ○ her ○ his	○ ○ ●
○ ○ ●	c) Ben: "Linda, here is ___ pen!" Linda: "Thank you!"	○ hers ○ yours ○ your	h) Joe: "Whose jacket is this?" Linda: "Oh! That is ___!"	○ mine ○ my ○ your	● ○ ○
○ ○ ●	d) Joe: "Is this Jenny's bag?" Katja: "Yes, that is ___ bag."	○ my ○ hers ○ her	i) Bob: "Is this Tim and Peter's ball?" Jill: "Yes, it's ___."	○ his ○ theirs ○ their	○ ● ○
○ ● ○	e) Sarah: "Are these our tickets?" Tom: "Yes, those are ___."	○ mine ○ ours ○ our	j) Ed: "Where are my parents' keys?" Sue: "Here are ___ keys."	○ their ○ theirs ○ yours	● ○ ○

Present Perfect – Positive statements with regular verbs ("verb-ed")

Form positive statements! Say what these people have just done.

Example: We ___ our mum.	○ has visited ● have visited	He ___ our mum.	● has visited ○ have visited
a) They _____ the car.	○ have cleaned (1a) ○ has cleaned (2a)	e) The guests _____ at the party.	○ has arrived (1e) ○ have arrived (2e)
b) Jill and Tim _____ for an hour.	○ have waited (1b) ○ has waited (2b)	f) My friend _____ a new job.	○ have started (1f) ○ has started (2f)
c) My sister _____ how to read.	○ have learned (1c) ○ has learned (2c)	g) I _____ my jacket twice.	○ have washed (1g) ○ has washed (2g)
d) The rain _____ !	○ have stopped (1d) ○ has stopped (2d)	h) They _____ here before.	○ has worked (1h) ○ have worked (2h)

Answers: 1a – 1b – 2c – 2d – 2e – 2f – 1g – 2h   Turn over!

Present Perfect – Positive statements with regular verbs ("verb-ed")

Form positive statements. Say what these people have just done.
Choose a verb from the verb box that fits.

Example: He ___ here. We ___ together.	→ He <u>has waited</u> here. → We <u>have waited</u> together.

	finish – visit – wash – talk – help – clean		open – stop – paint – start – repair – miss	
Fold back!				*Fold back!*
have visited	a) I _____ grandma at home.	g) The policeman _____ the car.		has stopped
has finished	b) Tim _____ work.	h) I _____ my bike.		have repaired
have talked	c) You _____ to her on the phone.	i) She _____ the window.		has opened
has helped	d) He _____ Tina with her homework.	j) It _____ to snow.		has started
have cleaned	e) The girls _____ their room.	k) The boys _____ the bus.		have missed
has washed	f) Linda _____ her jacket.	l) We _____ the wall.		have painted

Present Perfect – Positive statements with regular verbs ("verb-ed")

Form positive statements! Choose a verb that fits and say what these people have just done.

Example: We have _listened_ to him.

has cooked	a) My dad _____ dinner.		e) I _____ the floor.	have cleaned
have laughed	b) They _____ about the film.		f) She _____ him.	has stopped
have closed	c) You _____ the door.		g) They _____ football.	have played
has washed	d) He _____ his hands.		h) He _____ the window.	has opened

---

Present Perfect – Positive statements with irregular verbs

Form positive statements! Say what these people have just done.

	Example: He _____ a letter.	○ have written ● has written	We have _____ a letter.	● have written ○ has written	
● ○	a) They _____ 4 postcards.	○ have written ○ has written	f) My brother _____ his arm.	○ have broken ○ has broken	○ ●
○ ●	b) Peter _____ a great film.	○ have seen ○ has seen	g) My friends _____ my mum.	○ have met ○ has met	● ○
○ ●	c) My friend _____ too much lemonade.	○ have drunk ○ has drunk	h) We _____ our keys.	○ have lost ○ has lost	● ○
● ○	d) I _____ my girlfriend a rose.	○ have bought ○ has bought	i) My sister _____ a bike accident.	○ have had ○ has had	○ ●
○ ●	e) She _____ a funny book.	○ have read ○ has read	j) My dad _____ the car.	○ has sold ○ have sold	● ○

Present Perfect – Positive statements with irregular verbs

Form positive statements! Say what these people have just done.
Choose a verb from the verb box that fits.

Example: We _____ a letter.   → We <u>have written</u> a letter.
He _____ a letter.   → He <u>has written</u> a letter.

	start – lose – break – miss – go – do		play – catch – go – phone – eat – see	
have broken	a) I _____ my leg.	g)	Tim _____ out.	has gone
have gone	b) Peter and Tim _____ home.	h)	We _____ a pizza.	have eaten
have missed	c) You _____ Peter.	i)	She _____ a mouse.	has seen
has done	d) He _____ his homework.	j)	I _____ my friend.	have phoned
has started	e) It _____ to rain.	k)	The boys _____ .	have played
has lost	f) He _____ his keys.	l)	The policeman _____ the thief.	has caught

---

Present Perfect – Positive statements with irregular verbs

Form positive statements! Choose a verb that fits and say what these people have just done.

Example: We <u>listen</u> to you.

have stood	a) I _____ up.	e)	I _____ a letter.	have written
has had	b) He _____ an idea.	f)	Tom _____ his bike.	has ridden
have run	c) They _____ a race.	g)	Peter _____ his arm.	has broken
has thrown	d) He _____ the ball.	h)	I _____ my homework.	have done

Present Perfect and adverbs of frequency – Activity: Cutting out

> Die Signalwörter „already", „just", „never" stehen in der Regel vor dem Verb (past participle).

Cut out the word boxes and put the parts into the correct order.

Example: | already | I | have | Tina | invited. |
| I | have | already | invited | Tina. |

the bus (1a)	they (1b)	missed (1c)	have (1d)	just (1e)
have (2a)	been (2b)	never (2c)	I (2d)	to France (2e)
he (3a)	already (3b)	has (3c)	done (3d)	his homework (3e)
just (4a)	Linda (4b)	lost (4c)	has (4d)	her keys (4e)
the policeman (5a)	caught (5b)	already (5c)	has (5d)	the thief (5e)
to rain (6a)	started (6b)	has (6c)	just (6d)	It (6e)
a kangaroo (7a)	have (7b)	we (7c)	never (7d)	seen (7e)
just (8a)	written (8b)	I (8c)	have (8d)	a letter (8e)
Linda (9a)	the door (9b)	already (9c)	opened (9d)	has (9e)
Peter (10a)	never (10b)	eaten (10c)	has (10d)	a coconut (10e)
have (11a)	their work (11b)	finished (11c)	they (11d)	already (11e)
I (12a)	seen (12b)	have (12c)	just (12d)	a mouse (12e)

Answers:
1b-1d-1e-1c-1a / 2d-2a-2c-2b-2e / 3a-3c-3b-3d-3e / 4b-4d-4a-4c-4e / 5a-5d-5c-5b-5e / 6e-6c-6d-6b-6a / 7c-7b-7d-7e-7a / 8c-8d-8a-8b-8e / 9a-9e-9c-9d-9b / 10a-10d-10b-10c-10e / 11d-11a-11e-11c-11b / 12a-12c-12d-12b-12e

Turn over!

Present Perfect – Negative statements

Form negative statements!

> Für die Verneinung im Present Perfect gilt:
> **haven't + verb (past participle)**
> **hasn't + verb (past participle)**

Example:
I have bought a present. → I **haven't bought** a present.
He has bought a present. → He **hasn't bought** a present.

Fold back!

a) She has made a cake. →	She		a cake.	She hasn't made a cake.
b) We have done our work. →	We		our work.	We haven't done our work.
c) Peter has found the key. →	Peter		the key.	Peter hasn't found the key.
d) It has started to snow. →	It		to snow.	It hasn't started to snow.
e) They have run home. →	They			They haven't run home.
f) I have missed the train. →				I haven't missed the train.
g) Linda has gone to a party. →				Linda hasn't gone to the party.
h) The policeman has stopped her. →				The policeman hasn't stopped her.
i) The pupils have waited. →				The pupils haven't waited.

Present Perfect – Negative statements

Form negative statements!

> Für die Verneinung im Present Perfect gilt:
> **haven't + verb (past participle)**
> **hasn't + verb (past participle)**

Example:
I have bought a present. → I **haven't bought** a present.
He has bought a present. → He **hasn't bought** a present.

Fold back!

a) We have bought a new CD. →				We haven't bought a new CD.
b) They have taken a test. →				They haven't taken a test.
c) Mike has watched TV. →				Mike hasn't watched TV.
d) I have written a letter. →				I haven't written a letter.
e) My friend has flown to Paris. →				My friend hasn't flown to Paris.
f) Linda has called her friend. →				Linda hasn't called her friend.
g) My father repaired my bike. →				My father hasn't repaired my bike.
h) The thief has stolen a wallet. →				The thief hasn't stolen a wallet.
i) My sister has gone home. →				My sister hasn't gone home.

Present Perfect – Negative statements

a) Put the verb into the Present Perfect and form negative statements!

> Für die Verneinung im Present Perfect gilt:
> **haven't + verb (past participle)**
> **hasn't + verb (past participle)**

Example:
I have bought a present. → I <u>haven't bought</u> a present.
He has bought a present. → He <u>hasn't bought</u> a present.

					Fold back!
a) They (not buy) a new car. →					They haven't bought a new car.
b) Peter (not repair) the car. →					Peter hasn't repaired the car.
c) I (not send) an e-mail. →					I haven't sent an e-mail.
d) Linda (not write) a story. →					Linda hasn't written a story.
e) We (not have) lunch. →					We haven't had lunch.
f) She (not start) the engine. →					She hasn't started the engine.
g) I (not listen) to my new CD. →					I haven't listened to my new CD.
h) They (not watch) a DVD. →					They haven't watched a DVD.

b) Form positive and negative statements!
Say what these people have done and what they haven't done.

Example: ⊕ ⊖
I <u>have bought</u> some milk but I <u>haven't bought</u> any coffee <u>yet</u>.
He <u>has repaired</u> the bike but he <u>hasn't repaired</u> the door bell <u>yet</u>.

Fold back!

1. see: I _____ _____ Tom but I _____ _____ Linda yet.
   — have seen – haven't seen

2. do: He _____ _____ his Maths homework but he _____ _____ his English homework yet.
   — has done – hasn't done

3. clean: You _____ _____ the kitchen but you _____ _____ the bathroom _____ .
   — have cleaned – haven't cleaned … yet

4. visit: I _____ _____ my grandparents but I _____ _____ my aunt _____ .
   — have visited – haven't visited … yet

5. eat: They _____ _____ lunch but they _____ _____ the dessert _____ .
   — have eaten – haven't eaten … yet

6. invite: Linda _____ _____ Sarah to her party but she _____ _____ Tom _____ .
   — has invited – hasn't invited … yet

Present Perfect – Questions with "Have ...?" / "Has ...?"

Form questions!

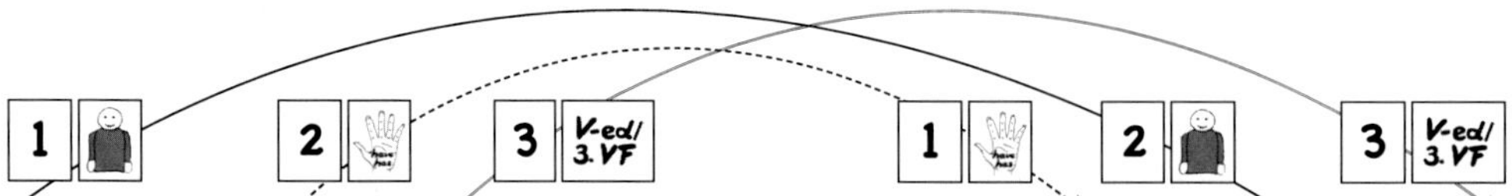

You	have	seen	Tina.	→	Have	you	seen	Tina?
He	has	seen	Tina.	→	Has	he	seen	Tina?
My brother	has	watched	TV.	→				
They	have	showed	her around.	→				
You	have	worked	on a project.	→				
The girls	have	gone	shopping.	→				
The pupils	have	done	their homework.	→				
I	have	locked	the door.	→				
Peter	has	eaten	a sandwich.	→				
My mother	has	talked	to the teacher.	→				
Our friends	have	visited	a museum.	→				
Lynn	has	had	lunch.	→				
They	have	been	to the cinema.	→				
The dog	has	chased	the cat.	→				
She	has	bought	a dress.	→				
The teacher	has	asked	a question.	→				

Answers:

1. Has your brother watched TV?
2. Have they showed her around?
3. Have you worked on a project?
4. Have the girls gone shopping?
5. Have the pupils done their homework?
6. Have I / you locked the door?
7. Has Peter eaten a sandwich?
8. Has my mother talked to the teacher?
9. Have our friends visited a museum?
10. Has Lynn had lunch?
11. Have they been to the cinema?
12. Has the dog chased the cat?
13. Has she bought a dress?
14. Has the teacher asked a question?

Turn over!

Present Perfect – Questions with "Have …?" / "Has …?"

Form questions! Fill in the correct form: "Have" or "Has".

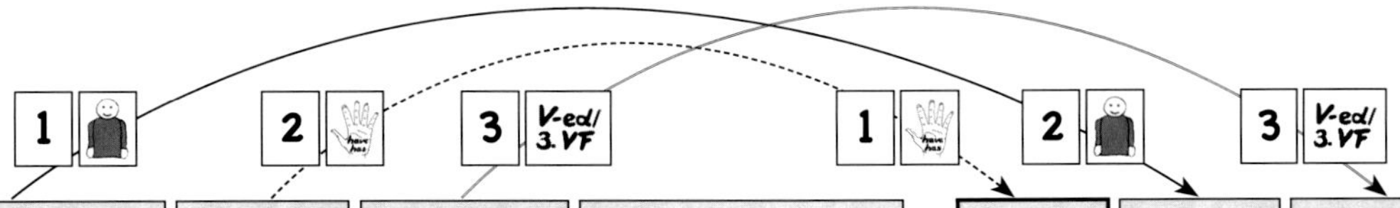

You	(have)	seen	Tina.	→	Have	you	seen	Tina?
He	(have)	seen	Tina.	→	Has	he	seen	Tina?
She	(have)	been	there.	→				
You	(have)	waited	for me.	→				
Tim	(have)	repaired	his bike.	→				
You	(have)	listened	to the new CD.	→				
Lynn	(have)	cleaned	her room.	→				
His friend	(have)	helped	them.	→				
They	(have)	gone	to the party.	→				
Your mother	(have)	cooked	for us.	→				
The policeman	(have)	arrested	the thief.	→				
The pupils	(have)	finished	their work.	→				
It	(have)	started	to rain.	→				
You	(have)	broken	the glass.	→				
Our friends	(have)	arrived	at the cinema.	→				
My father	(have)	bought	the house.	→				

Answers:

1. Has she been there?
2. Have you waited for me?
3. Has Tim repaired his bike?
4. Have you listened to the new CD?
5. Has Lynn cleaned her room?
6. Has his friend helped them?
7. Have they gone to the party?
8. Has your mother cooked for us?
9. Has the policeman arrested the thief?
10. Have the pupils finished their work?
11. Has it started to rain?
12. Have you broken the glass?
13. Have our friends arrived at the cinema?
14. Has my father bought the house?

 Turn over!

Present Perfect – Questions with "Have …?" / "Has …?"

Form questions! Fill in the correct past participle of the verb in brackets!

You	have	(see)	Tina.	→	Have	you	seen	Tina?
He	has	(see)	Tina.	→	Has	he	seen	Tina?
The pupils	have	(do)	their homework.	→				
You	have	(leave)	the party.	→				
The teacher	has	(plan)	a school trip.	→				
They	have	(take)	the test.	→				
Peter	has	(meet)	her.	→				

Now also choose the correct form: "Have" or "Has"!

Lynn	(have)	(read)	a book.	→				
Your father	(have)	(leave)	the house.	→				
They	(have)	(hear)	a noise.	→				
The man	(have)	(send)	an e-mail.	→				
We	(have)	(pay)	for the food.	→				
The policeman	(have)	(stop)	the car.	→				
The women	(have)	(laugh)	a lot.	→				
Dave	(have)	(have)	breakfast.	→				
The mice	(have)	(eat)	my cheese.	→				

Answers:
1. Have the pupils done their homework?
2. Have you left the party?
3. Has the teacher planned a school trip?
4. Have they taken the test?
5. Has Peter met her?
6. Has Lynn read a book?
7. Has your father left the house?
8. Have they heard a noise?
9. Has the man sent an e-mail?
10. Have we paid for the food?
11. Has the policeman stopped the car?
12. Have the women laughed a lot?
13. Has Dave had breakfast?
14. Have the mice eaten my cheese?

Turn over!

Present Perfect – Questions and short answers with "have" / "has"

Mark the correct answer!

Example:
I have seen him already.
Have you seen him yet?   ● Yes, I have.   ○ No, I haven't.

● a) Peter has just bought a new bike.   ○ Yes, he has.
○   Has Peter bought a new bike yet?   ○ No, he hasn't.

○ b) They have just walked to school.   ○ Yes, they have.
●   Have they walked home?   ○ No, they haven't.

○ c) She has just gone to the doctor.   ○ Yes, she has.
●   Has she gone to the cinema?   ○ No, she hasn't.

● d) It has started to rain.   ○ Yes, it has.
○   Has it started to rain yet?   ○ No, it hasn't.

● e) My friends have prepared lunch.   ○ Yes, they have.
○   Have your friends prepared lunch?   ○ No, they haven't.

● f) Mr Smith has talked to my mum.   ○ Yes, he has.
○   Has Mr Smith talked to your mum?   ○ No, he hasn't.

g) He has watched TV.   ○ Yes, he has.   ●
   Has he watched TV?   ○ No, he hasn't.   ○

h) I haven't eaten lunch yet.   ○ Yes, I have.   ○
   Have you eaten lunch yet?   ○ No, I haven't.   ●

i) Sue hasn't called John.   ○ Yes, she has.   ○
   Has Sue called John yet?   ○ No, she hasn't.   ●

j) It hasn't worked yet.   ○ Yes, it has.   ○
   Has it worked yet?   ○ No, it hasn't.   ●

k) I have bought a burger.   ○ Yes, I have.   ○
   Have you bought a soup?   ○ No, I haven't.   ●

l) They haven't met Peter.   ○ Yes, they have.   ○
   Have they met Peter?   ○ No, they haven't.   ●

Present Perfect – Questions and short answers with "have" / "has"

Give a short answer!

Example: I have already seen him.
Have you seen him yet?   →   <u>Yes, I have.</u>

a) Lynn hasn't done her homework yet. Has Lynn done her homework yet?	→ No, she _____	No, she hasn't.
b) They have just left the party. Have they just arrived at the party?	→ No, they _____	No, they haven't.
c) Peter has taken the dog for a walk. Has Peter taken the dog for a walk?	→ Yes, he _____	Yes, he has.
d) It has started to rain. Has it started to snow yet?	→ _____	No, it hasn't.
e) My friends have missed the bus. Have your friends just missed the bus?	→ _____	Yes, they have.
f) Mr Brown has just talked to my dad. Has Mr Brown just talked to your dad?	→ _____	Yes, he has.
g) I have watched TV. Have you watched TV?	→ _____	Yes, I have.
h) He has just eaten a sandwich. Has he just eaten a cake?	→ _____	No, he hasn't.

Present Perfect – Questions and short answers with "have" / "has"

Give a short answer!

Example: I have seen him already.
Have you seen him yet? → <u>Yes, I have</u>.

			Fold back!
a) Have you just done your homework?	→	_____	Yes, I have. / No, I haven't. /
b) Have you just read this question?	→	_____	Yes, I have.
c) Has your teacher just given you this worksheet?	→	_____	Yes, she / he has. / No, she / he hasn't.
d) Has it started to rain yet?	→	_____	No, it hasn't. / Yes, it has.
e) Have you already had breakfast?	→	_____	Yes, I have. / No, I haven't.
f) Has a mouse just run through the room?	→	_____	No, it hasn't.
g) Has your classmate just talked to you?	→	_____	Yes, she / he has. / No, she / he hasn't.
h) Have your classmates just run around?	→	_____	Yes, they have. / No, they haven't.

Present Perfect – Questions with question words

Form questions! Find the correct order!

Example:

you	have	seen	who	→	Who	have	you	seen?
he	has	seen	who	→	Who	has	he	seen?

Peter	gone?	where	has	→				
have	you	bought?	which bike	→				
whose pen	have	I	broken?	→				
done?	what	has	my brother	→				
has	he	why	shouted?	→				

Now also choose the correct form: "have" or "has"!

who	met?	you	(have)	→				
drunk?	he	(have)	how much	→				
(have)	the cat	where	been?	→				
how many	(have)	counted?	you	→				
(have)	what	done?	my father	→				
where	you	(have)	been?	→				
how much	(have)	paid?	my mother	→				
stopped?	why	it	(have)	→				
the teacher	what	(have)	said?	→				

Answers:

1. Where has Peter gone?
2. Which bike have you bought?
3. Whose pen have I broken?
4. What has my brother done?
5. Why has he shouted?
6. Who have you met?
7. How much has he drunk?
8. Where has the cat been?
9. How many have you counted?
10. What has my father done?
11. Where have you been?
12. How much has my mother paid?
13. Why has it stopped?
14. What has the teacher said?

Turn over!

Present Perfect – Questions with question words

Form questions in the Present Perfect!
Find the correct order and choose the correct form: "have" or "has"!

Example:

				→	?	have/has	😊	V-ed/3.VF
you	(have)	seen	who	→	Who	have	you	seen?
he	(have)	seen	who	→	Who	has	he	seen?
stolen	they	(have)	whose car	→				
what	bought	Paula	(have)	→				
you	(have)	bought	which jacket	→				
(have)	why	called	Mike	→				
what	he	(have)	done	→				

Now also choose the correct past participle form of the verb!

				→				
(be)	(have)	where	my sister	→				
why	the dog	(have)	(bark)	→				
(have)	you	(pay)	how much	→				
(buy)	(have)	you	which present	→				
the pupils	(play)	(have)	where	→				
(have)	they	how often	(write)	→				
why	they	(finish)	(have)	→				
the policeman	who	(have)	(arrest)	→				
where	(have)	(go)	my friends	→				

Answers:
1. Whose car have they stolen?
2. What has Paula bought?
3. Which jacket have you bought?
4. Why has Mike called?
5. What has he done?
6. Where has my sister been?
7. Why has the dog barked?
8. How much have you paid?
9. Which present have you bought?
10. Where have the pupils played?
11. How often have they written?
12. Why have they finished?
13. Who has the policeman arrested?
14. Where have my friends gone?

Present Perfect – Questions with question words

Form questions in the Present Perfect!
Choose "have" or "has" and the correct past participle form!

Example:

you	(have)	(see)	who	→	Who	have	you	seen?
he	(have)	(see)	who	→	Who	has	he	seen?
(have)	(do)	you	what	→				
(go)	he	(have)	where	→				
(book)	(have)	we	which hotel	→				
where	(run)	(have)	the dog	→				
(steal)	(have)	they	whose bike	→				
how many	Peter	(make)	(have)	→				
what	(buy)	(have)	my mother	→				
how often	(have)	he	(phone)	→				
(have)	the cat	(jump)	where	→				
(lose)	(have)	Tina	which key	→				
how much	(write)	(have)	the pupils	→				
how	(have)	(be)	your uncle	→				
they	why	(have)	(fight)	→				
which cake	you	(make)	(have)	→				

Answers:

1. What have you done?
2. Where has he gone?
3. Which hotel have we booked?
4. Where has the dog run?
5. Whose bike have they stolen?
6. How many has Peter made?
7. What has my mother bought?
8. How often has he phoned?
9. Where has the cat jumped?
10. Which key has Tina lost?
11. How much have the pupils written?
12. How has your uncle been?
13. Why have they fought?
14. Which cake have you made?

Turn over!

Question tags

Tick the correct question tag!

Example: Peter is here, ⊕ ⊖ ___? ○ is he ● isn't he

You aren't angry, ⊖ ⊕ ___? ● are you ○ aren't you

● a) You are tired, ⊕ ⊖ ___? ○ aren't you ○ are you
○

● b) Mike isn't here, ⊖ ⊕ ___? ○ is he ○ isn't he
○

○ c) Lisa is hungry, ⊕ ⊖ ___? ○ is she ○ isn't she
●

d) Sue and Jerry aren't friends, ⊖ ⊕ ___? ○ are they ○ aren't they ●
○

e) This pen is yours, ⊕ ⊖ ___? ○ is it ○ isn't it ○
●

f) This shirt isn't mine, ⊖ ⊕ ___? ○ is it ○ isn't it ●
○

Question tags

Finish the sentences with the correct question tag!

Example: Peter is here, ⊕ ⊖ _isn't_ he?

You aren't angry, ⊖ ⊕ _are_ you?

isn't — a) Lynn is a new pupil, ⊕ ⊖ _____ she?

aren't — b) The girls are tired, ⊕ ⊖ _____ they?

isn't — c) This jacket is yours, ⊕ ⊖ _____ it?

d) The boys aren't here, ⊖ ⊕ _____ they? — *are*

e) The bag isn't mine, ⊖ ⊕ _____ it? — *is*

f) You are tired, ⊕ ⊖ _____ you? — *aren't*

Question tags

Finish the sentences with the correct personal pronoun and a correct question tag!

Example: Peter is here, ⊕ ⊖ _isn't he_?

You aren't angry, ⊖ ⊕ _are you_?

is he — a) Till isn't angry, ⊖ ⊕ _____ _____?

aren't we — b) We are early, ⊕ ⊖ _____ _____?

aren't they — c) Our pets are cute, ⊕ ⊖ _____ _____?

isn't it — d) This scarf is yours, ⊕ ⊖ _____ _____?

e) Your parents aren't here, ⊖ ⊕ ____ ___? — *are they*

f) My brother is cool, ⊕ ⊖ _____ _____? — *isn't he*

g) Mum isn't at home, ⊖ ⊕ _____ _____? — *is she*

h) Rita is from Germany, ⊕ ⊖ _____ _____? — *isn't she*

The going to-future – Positive statements

Das going to-future verwendest du bei festen Plänen und Absichten der Zukunft:
am / is / are + going to + infinitive

a) Mark the correct form of the going-to future!

I / He / We ...	am / is / are	+ going to	+ infinitive
Example: She	_____	+ _____	+ _____ Tom	○ are going to see ● is going to see

a) I _____ a book.
○ am going to read (g)
○ is going to read (e)
○ are going to read (w)

b) Peter and Tim _____ TV.
○ am going to watch (t)
○ is going to watch (d)
○ are going to watch (r)

c) He _____ some friends.
○ am going to meet (t)
○ is going to meet (e)
○ are going to meet (o)

d) We _____ lunch.
○ am going to have (W)
○ is going to have (h)
○ are going to have (a)

e) Mrs Smith _____ a car.
○ am going to buy (e)
○ is going to buy (t)
○ are going to buy (p)

f) They _____ a race.
○ am going to run (d)
○ is going to run (o)
○ are going to run (j)

g) Peter _____ an e-mail.
○ am going to send (s)
○ is going to send (o)
○ are going to send (n)

h) She _____ on holiday.
○ am going to go (a)
○ is going to go (b)
○ are going to go (j)

Write down the letter behind each answer. Keep to the order a, b, c …
If your answers are correct, you can read your code: ___ ___ ___ ___ ___ ___ ___ ___ !

b) Now you! Put the verb into the going to-future!

Example:	👤	am/is/are	going to	✓		
write:	He	is	going to	write	a letter.	
a) clean:	Mum	is		clean	the kitchen.	… (is) going to (clean) …
b) visit:	They	are			their uncle.	… (are) going to visit …
c) phone:	I				my friend.	… am going to phone …
d) go:	Jenny				to university.	… is going to go …
e) study:	My friend				in France.	… is going to study …
f) watch:	They				a match.	… are going to watch …
g) have:	We				breakfast.	… are going to have …
h) buy:	She				a CD.	… is going to buy …
i) meet:	I				my friends.	… am going to meet …

Fold back!

The going to-future – Positive statements

Das going to-future verwendest du bei festen Plänen und Absichten der Zukunft:
am / is / are + going to + infinitive

Put the verb in the going to-future!

Example:						
write:	He	is	going	to	write	a letter.
go:	We	are	going	to	go	to London.
a) read:	Sally	is			read	a magazine.	… (is) going to (read) …
b) watch:	They	are			watch	a DVD.	… (are) going to (watch) …
c) meet:	I	am			meet	a friend.	… (am) going to (meet) …
d) go:	We					to the cinema.	… are going to go …
e) buy:	Tom					a new shirt.	… is going to buy …
f) stay:	My parents					at a hotel.	… are going to stay …
g) have:	I					dinner.	… am going to have …
h) steal:	The thief					the painting.	… is going to steal …
i) leave:	We					the party soon.	… are going to leave …
j) ask:	He					his teacher.	… is going to ask …
k) swim:	They					in the river.	… are going to swim …
l) plan:	My friends					their holiday.	… are going to plan …
m) do:	I					some exercise.	… am going to do …
n) play:	Sue and Jim					tennis.	… are going to play …
o) talk:	Mike					to his teacher.	… is going to talk …
p) paint:	Lynn					her room.	… is going to paint …
q) wash:	I					my jacket.	… am going to wash …
r) be:	They					on time.	… are going to be …

64 Freiarbeitsmaterialien für die 6. Klasse: Englisch

© scolix

The going to-future – Positive statements

Das going to-future verwendest du bei festen Plänen und Absichten der Zukunft:
am / is / are + going to + infinitive

a) Put the verb into the going to-future!

Example:	😊	am is are	going to	✓	
write:	He	is	going to	write	a letter.
go:	We	are	going to	go	to London.
a) meet:	I				my sister. … am going to meet …
b) take:	Peter				the exam. … is going to take …
c) clean:	My mum				the kitchen. … is going to clean …
d) go:	We				to the zoo. … are going to go …
e) help:	Linda				her mother. … is going to help …
f) wash:	I				my dress. … am going to wash …
g) talk:	My parents				to my teacher. … are going to talk …

b) Choose a correct verb from the verb box and put it in the going to-future!

Example:	😊	am is are	going to	✓	
write:	He	is	going to	write	a letter.

have – go – buy – read – listen – eat – do – learn

a)	My brother				a new shirt. … is going to buy …
b)	We				to the cinema. … are going to go …
c)	Lynn				a book. … is going to read …
d)	I				to my new CD. … am going to listen …
e)	They				breakfast. … are going to have …
f)	Dave				his homework. … is going to do …
g)	I				a pizza. … am going to eat …
h)	The choir				a new song. … is going to learn …

The going to-future – Negative statements (long form)

	I / He / We ...	am / is / are	not	+	going to	+	infinitive	
Example:	She	is	*		going to		see	Tom.
	She	is	not		going to		see	Tom.

Form negative statements!

1. We are * going to wait for him. → _____
2. My parents are * going to go home. → _____
3. My friend is * going to read a book. → _____
4. Our aunt is * going to visit us. → _____
5. The pupils are * going to have lunch. → _____
6. My sister is * going to help me. → _____
7. I am * going to go to bed. → _____
8. They are * going to work hard. → _____
9. He is * going to sleep on the sofa. → _____
10. My friends are * going to watch TV. → _____
11. I am * going to meet her. → _____
12. We are * going to swim in the sea. → _____
13. Lynn is * going to drive the new car. → _____
14. The Millers are * going to travel a lot. → _____
15. Peter is * going to listen to a new CD. → _____
16. We are * going to play football. → _____

Answers:
1. *We are not going to wait for him.*
2. *My parents are not going to go home.*
3. *My friend is not going to read a book.*
4. *Our aunt is not going to visit us.*
5. *The pupils are not going to have lunch.*
6. *My sister is not going to help me.*
7. *I am not going to go to bed.*
8. *They are not going to work hard.*
9. *He is not going to sleep on the sofa.*
10. *My friends are not going to watch TV.*
11. *I am not going to meet her.*
12. *We are not going to swim in the sea.*
13. *Lynn is not going to drive the new car.*
14. *The Millers are not going to travel a lot.*
15. *Peter is not going to listen to a new CD.*
16. *We are not going to play football.*

Turn over!

The going to-future – Negative statements (long form)

Form negative statements!

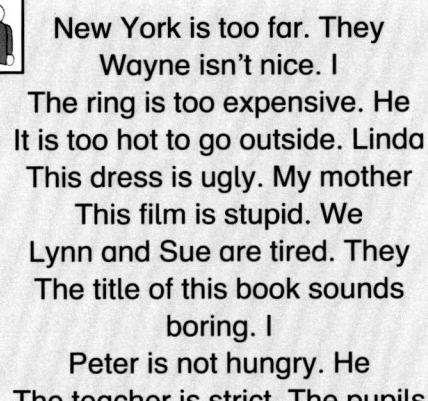

	am / is / are	not	going to	✓
New York is too far. They	am	not	going to	read it.
Wayne isn't nice. I	is			travel there.
The ring is too expensive. He	are			leave the house.
It is too hot to go outside. Linda				watch it.
This dress is ugly. My mother				have lunch.
This film is stupid. We				do their homework.
Lynn and Sue are tired. They				run around.
The title of this book sounds boring. I				buy it for her.
Peter is not hungry. He				wear it.
The teacher is strict. The pupils				help him.

1. _____
2. _____
3. _____
4. _____
5. _____
6. _____
7. _____
8. _____
9. _____
10. _____

Answers:

1. New York is too far. They are not going to travel there.
2. Wayne isn't nice. I am not going to help him.
3. The ring is too expensive. He is not going to buy it for her.
4. It is too hot to go outside. Linda is not going to leave the house.
5. This dress is ugly. My mother is not going to wear it.
6. This film is stupid. We are not going to watch it.
7. Lynn and Sue are tired. They are not going to do their homework.
8. The title of this book sounds boring. I am not going to read it.
9. Peter is not hungry. He is not going to have lunch.
10. The teacher is strict. The pupils are not going to run around.

The going to-future – Negative statements (long form)

	I / He / We ...	am / is / are	not	+	going to	+	infinitive	
Example:	She	is	*		going to		see	Tom.
	She	is	**not**		going to		see	Tom.

Form negative statements!

Example: read: I <u>am not going to read</u> this book.
           repair: We <u>are not going to repair</u> the car.

1. phone: They _____ their parents.

2. eat: We _____ pizza for dinner.

3. clean: My father _____ the dirty car.

4. drive: I _____ your new car.

5. buy: Tom _____ a new shirt.

6. watch: We _____ a DVD.

7. wait: They _____ for you.

8. go: My friends and I _____ to a disco.

9. ride: She _____ Tom's bike.

10. work: I _____ a lot on Sunday.

11. have: My parents _____ breakfast.

12. wash: My mum _____ my shirt.

13. take: Peter _____ the dog for a walk.

14. talk: Tom and John _____ to Linda.

15. run: The pupils _____ around in class.

16. sleep: I _____ on the sofa when there is a bed.

Answers:

1. They are not going to phone ...
2. We are not going to eat ...
3. My father is not going to clean ...
4. I am not going to drive ...
5. Tom is not going to buy ...
6. We are not going to watch ...
7. They are not going to wait ...
8. My friends and I are not going to go ...
9. She is not going to ride ...
10. I am not going to work ...
11. My parents are not going to have ...
12. My mum is not going to wash ...
13. Peter is not going to take ...
14. Tom and John are not going to talk ...
15. The pupils are not going to run ...
16. I am not going to sleep ...

Turn over!

The going to-future – Negative statements (short form)

	I / He / We ...	'm not / isn't / aren't	+	going to	+	infinitive	
Example:	She	is		going to		see	Tom.
	She	isn't		going to		see	Tom.

Form negative statements! Choose 'm not, isn't or aren't.

1. We * going to play tennis. → ___
2. My parents * going to have dinner. → ___
3. My friend * going to buy a new dress. → ___
4. Our aunt * going to travel to the USA. → ___
5. The pupils * going to go on a bike trip. → ___
6. My brother * going to repair my bike. → ___
7. I * going to watch TV. → ___
8. They * going to work hard. → ___
9. He * going to wait for her. → ___
10. My friends * going to go out. → ___
11. I * going to phone him. → ___
12. We * going to have a party. → ___
13. Lynn * going to drive to the market. → ___
14. The Millers * going to buy a new car. → ___
15. Peter * going to visit his uncle. → ___
16. We * going to clean the kitchen. → ___

Answers:
1. We aren't going to play tennis.
2. My parents aren't going to have dinner.
3. My friend isn't going to buy a new dress.
4. Our aunt isn't going to travel to the USA.
5. The pupils aren't going to go on a bike trip.
6. My brother isn't going to repair my bike.
7. I'm not going to watch TV.
8. They aren't going to work hard.
9. He isn't going to wait for her.
10. My friends aren't going to go out.
11. I'm not going to phone him.
12. We aren't going to have a party.
13. Lynn isn't going to drive to the market.
14. The Millers aren't going to buy a new car.
15. Peter isn't going to visit his uncle.
16. We aren't going to clean the kitchen.

The going to-future – Negative statements (short form)

Form negative statements! Choose 'm not, isn't or aren't.

I haven't got any money left. I We don't like rap music. We My father has just cleaned the car. He Linda broke her leg. She Sue and John are in New York. They Tim has already seen the new film. He It's raining. We This book is boring. I The policemen are here. The thief John can't dance. He	'm not isn't aren't	 going to	watch the film with us. go to the disco with you. take part in the Judo class. be back before next week. go to the rap concert. steal any paintings. buy a new dress. read the end. walk in the park. clean it again.

1. _____
2. _____
3. _____
4. _____
5. _____
6. _____
7. _____
8. _____
9. _____
10. _____

Answers:

1. I haven't got any money left. I'm not going to buy a new dress.
2. We don't like rap music. We aren't going to go to the rap concert.
3. My father has just cleaned the car. He isn't going to clean it again.
4. Linda broke her leg. She isn't going to take part in the Judo class.
5. Sue and John are in New York. They aren't going to be back before next week.
6. Tim has already seen the new film. He isn't going to watch the film with us.
7. It's raining. We aren't going to walk in the park.
8. This book is boring. I'm not going to read the end.
9. The policemen are here. The thief isn't going to steal any paintings.
10. John can't dance. He isn't going to go to the disco with you.

 Turn over!

The going to-future – Negative statements (short form)

	I / He / We ...	'm not / isn't / aren't	+	going to	+	infinitive	
Example:	She	is		going to		see	Tom.
	She	isn't		going to		see	Tom.

Form negative statements using the short form!

Example: read: I 'm not going to read this book.
repair: We aren't going to repair the car.

1. play: They _____ football in the park.
2. meet: We _____ to work on our project again.
3. repair: My father _____ the old car.
4. ride: I _____ my new bike in the dirt.
5. watch: Tom _____ a DVD.
6. have: We _____ breakfast with my friends.
7. plan: They _____ a bike tour for tomorrow.
8. go: My friends and I _____ the party later.
9. wait: She _____ for her friend Tom.
10. buy: I _____ a new pullover.
11. stay: My parents _____ at a hotel.
12. clean: My mum _____ the kitchen alone.
13. phone: Peter _____ his uncle.
14. sleep: Tom and John _____ in a hostel.
15. go: The pupils _____ on a school trip tomorrow.
16. listen: I _____ to all these new CDs.

Answers:
1. They aren't going to play ...
2. We aren't going to meet ...
3. My father isn't going to repair ...
4. I'm not going to ride ...
5. Tom isn't going to watch ...
6. We aren't going to have ...
7. They aren't going to plan ...
8. My friends and I aren't going to go ...
9. She isn't going to wait ...
10. I'm not going to buy ...
11. My parents aren't going to stay ...
12. My mum isn't going to clean ...
13. Peter isn't going to phone ...
14. Tom and John aren't going to sleep ...
15. The pupils aren't going to go ...
16. I'm not going to listen ...

The going to-future – Questions

Form questions about what these people are going to do.

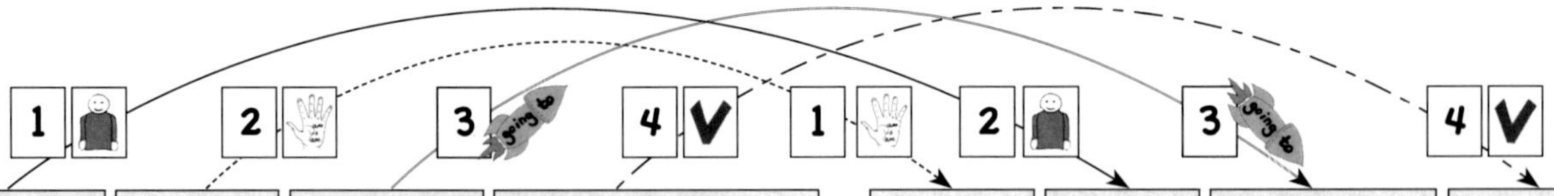

They	are	going to	leave.	Are	they	going to	leave?
He	is	going to	stay.	Is	he	going to	stay?

Tim	is	going to	work.				
They	are	going to	play.				
You	are	going to	move.				
She	is	going to	ask.				
I	am	going to	help.				
My dad	is	going to	start.				
We	are	going to	try.				
I	am	going to	finish.				
They	are	going to	eat.				
Lynn	is	going to	stay.				
Peter	is	going to	study.				
You	are	going to	phone.				

Answers:

1. Is Tim going to work?
2. Are they going to play?
3. Are you going to move?
4. Is she going to ask?
5. Am I going to help?
6. Is my dad going to start?
7. Are we going to try?
8. Am I going to finish?
9. Are they going to eat?
10. Is Lynn going to stay?
11. Is Peter going to study?
12. Are you going to phone?

The going to-future – Questions

Form questions about what these people are going to do.

Am / Is / Are			watch	it?
Mike has got a new bike. Is			read	it, too?
Tina bought a new dress. Is			take	a taxi instead?
I bought a new DVD for us. Are	it		ride	it for the bike tour?
Phil is a strong man. Is	we		wear	it for the party?
They are too late for the bus. Are	she	going	study	Maths at the university?
Linda's leg hurts. Is	they	to	clean	it?
Tom, this book is awesome! Are	he		see	a doctor?
Your brother is good at Maths. Is	you		work	properly?
Look at this dirty kitchen! Girls, are			carry	all the heavy boxes?
This machine looks strange. Is				

Example: _Are_   _you_   _going to_   _go home?_

1. _____
2. _____
3. _____
4. _____
5. _____
6. _____
7. _____
8. _____
9. _____
10. _____

Answers:

1. Mike has got a new bike. Is he going to ride it for the bike tour?
2. Tina bought a new dress. Is she going to wear it for the party?
3. I bought a new DVD for us. Are we going to watch it?
4. Phil is a strong man. Is he going to carry all the heavy boxes?
5. They are too late for the bus. Are they going to take a taxi instead?
6. Linda's leg hurts. Is she going to see a doctor?
7. Tom, this book is awesome! Are you going to read it, too?
8. Your brother is good at Maths. Is he going to study Maths at the university?
9. Look at this dirty kitchen! Girls, are you going to clean it?
10. This machine looks strange. Is it going to work properly?

Turn over!

The going to-future – Questions

Look at the pictures! Form questions about what these people are going to do tomorrow.

| They | are | going to | leave. | → | Are | they | going to | leave? |
| He | is | going to | stay. | → | Is | he | going to | stay? |

Example: Is he going to leave?

1. _____ he – leave
2. _____ she – have – a party
3. _____ he – clean – his room
4. _____ they – play – football
5. _____ you – ride – your bike
6. _____ they – meet
7. _____ they – listen – to the new CD
8. _____ you – go shopping
9. _____ your brother – wash – the car
10. _____ he – eat – at a restaurant
11. _____ he – write – a letter

Answers:
1. Is she going to have a party?
2. Is he going to clean his room?
3. Are they going to play football?
4. Are you going to ride your bike?
5. Are they going to meet?
6. Are they going to listen to the new CD?
7. Are you going to go shopping?
8. Is your brother going to wash the car?
9. Is he going to eat at a restaurant?
10. Is he going to write a letter?

Turn over!

The will-future

> Du verwendest das will-future für Zukünftiges, das du nicht beeinflussen kannst oder wenn du vermutest, dass etwas geschehen wird.
> **Beachte:** Nach „will" / „won't" folgt das Verb in der <u>Grundform</u>!
> I will <u>play</u>.

a) Fill in "will" + verb or "won't" + verb!

Sarah ✓ sing	Sarah	will sing	in a choir tomorrow.	
Linda ✗ sing	Linda	won't sing	in a choir tomorrow.	
Tim and Bill ✓ play	Tim and Bill	_____ play	a match tomorrow.	Tim and Bill will …
My father ✗ cook	My father	_____ cook	for us later.	My father won't …
Peter ✓ swim	Peter	_____ _____	in a team next month.	Peter will swim …
Linda ✓ dance	_____	_____ _____	at the disco tomorrow.	Linda will dance …
Bill ✗ drive	_____	_____ _____	us home later.	Bill won't drive …
My brother ✓ ride	_____	_____ _____	his new bike later.	My brother will ride …
He ✗ write	_____	_____ _____	a letter tomorrow.	He won't write …
Tom ✓ eat	_____	_____ _____	at a restaurant tomorrow.	Tom will eat …
I ✗ clean	_____	_____ _____	my room next week.	I won't clean …
Peter ✓ think	_____	_____ _____	about it later.	Peter will think …

b) Now you! Put the verb into the will-future! Use "will" or "won't"!

a) + meet: I _____ _____ her at the bus stop tomorrow. — will meet

b) + go: We _____ _____ to Spain next year. — will go

c) – buy: My father _____ _____ a new car. — won't buy

d) – move: My friend _____ _____ next month. — won't move

e) + help: Wait, I _____ _____ you. — will help

f) – visit: Peter _____ _____ his grandma next weekend. — won't visit

g) – give: She _____ _____ back your book before next Friday. — won't give

The will-future

Beachte: Nach „will" / „won't" folgt das Verb in der <u>Grundform</u>! I will <u>play</u>. / I won't <u>play</u>.

a) Fill in "will" + verb or "won't" + verb!

Sarah ✓ sing	Sarah	will sing	in a choir tomorrow.	
Linda ✗ sing	Linda	won't sing	in a choir tomorrow.	Fold back!
Tim and Bill ✓ play			football tomorrow.	Tim and Bill will play …
My father ✗ wash			the car next weekend.	My father won't wash …
Peter ✓ pay			later.	Peter will pay …
Linda ✗ have			a party for her birthday.	Linda won't have …
Bill ✓ show			us the way.	Bill will show …
My brother ✓ take			some photos.	My brother will take …
He ✗ go			by bus.	He won't go …
Tom ✓ phone			his girlfriend next week.	Tom will phone …
I ✗ go shopping			on Friday.	I won't go shopping …
Peter ✓ wait			for us.	Peter will wait …

b) Now you! Put the verb into the will-future! Use "will" or "won't"!

a) + call: We _____ _____ a taxi later. — *will call*

b) – be: It _____ _____ sunny tomorrow. — *won't be*

c) + send: My father _____ _____ us a postcard from Scotland. — *will send*

d) – have: They _____ _____ breakfast with their friends. — *won't have*

e) + like: I'm sure she _____ _____ this dress. — *will like*

f) – buy: My parents _____ _____ more sweets. — *won't buy*

The will-future

Beachte: Nach „will" / „won't" folgt das Verb in der <u>Grundform</u>! I will <u>play</u>. / I won't <u>play</u>.

a) Sort the letters for the verb and fill in "will" + verb or "won't" + verb!

n i g s	Sarah	*Sarah will sing tomorrow.*	
	Linda	*Linda won't sing tomorrow.*	
a w h s		Wait, I _____ my _____.	... I will wash my hands.
g u l a h		I am sure, he _____ at you.	... he won't laugh at you.
o d		Peter _____ his _____ later.	Peter will do his homework later.
d r e i		My father _____ his new bike later.	My father won't ride his new bike later.
d n c a e		Jenny _____ in a disco show tomorrow.	Jenny will dance ...

b) Choose a verb that fits and put the verb into the will-future! Use "will" or "won't"!

a) +: I think she _____ _____ a postcard from Italy.   *will send*

b) –: I'm sure we _____ _____ to the cinema next weekend.   *won't go*

c) +: Wait, don't do it on your own. I _____ _____ you!   *will help*

d) –: I think my parents _____ _____ at the restaurant tonight.   *won't eat*

e) –: I am sure they _____ _____ at a hotel tomorrow.   *won't stay / sleep*

f) +: Peter _____ _____ 16 years old next month.   *will be*

g) +: I hope he _____ _____ my new article in the magazine.   *will read*

h) –: They probably _____ _____ shopping tomorrow.   *won't go*

i) +: The car is very dirty. I think I _____ _____ it.   *will wash / clean*

j) –: I think he _____ _____ to the party. He is ill.   *won't come*

The will-future: Questions with "Will ...?"

a) Sort the word boxes and form questions with "will"!

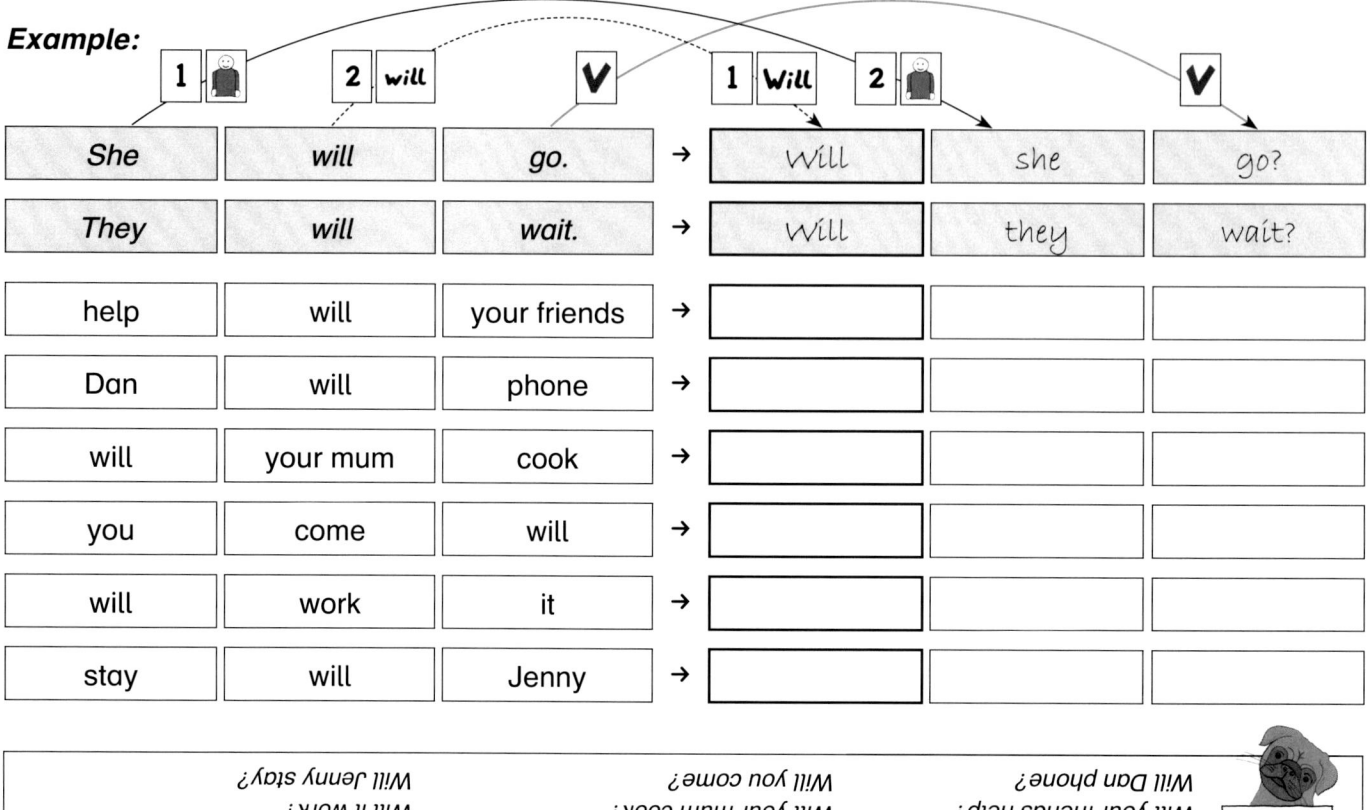

b) Sort the word boxes and form questions with a question word + "will"!

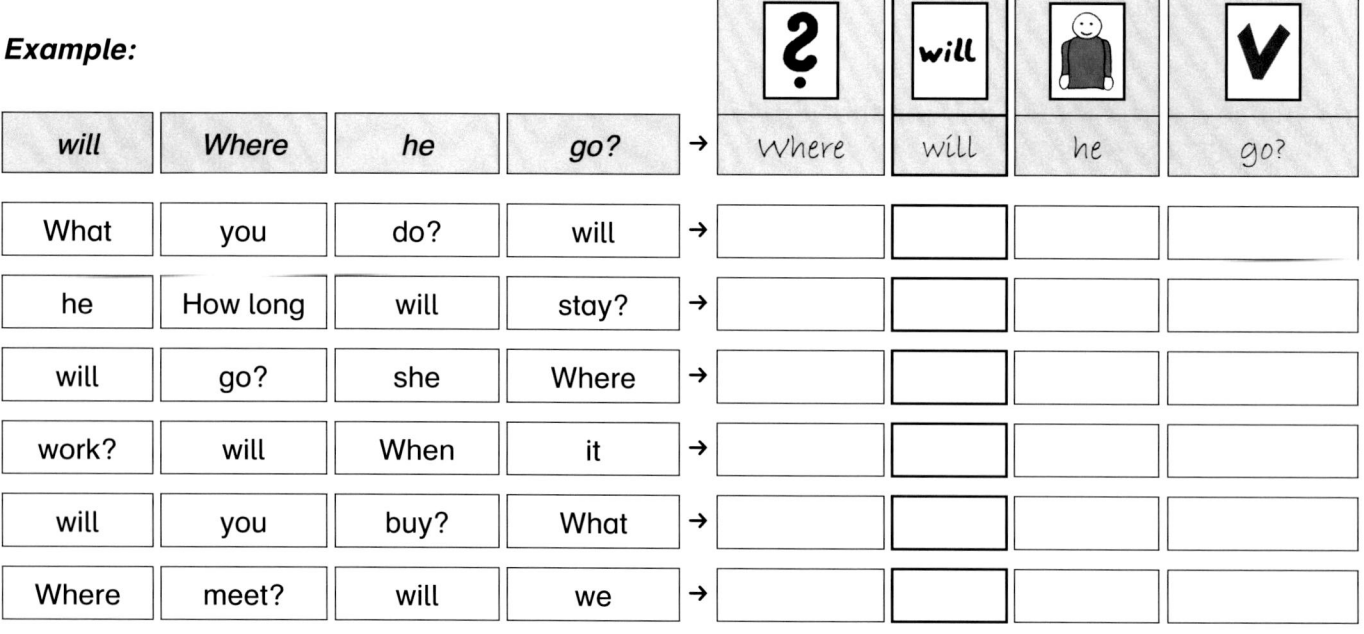

The will-future: Questions with "Will ...?"

a) Sort the word boxes and form questions with "will"!

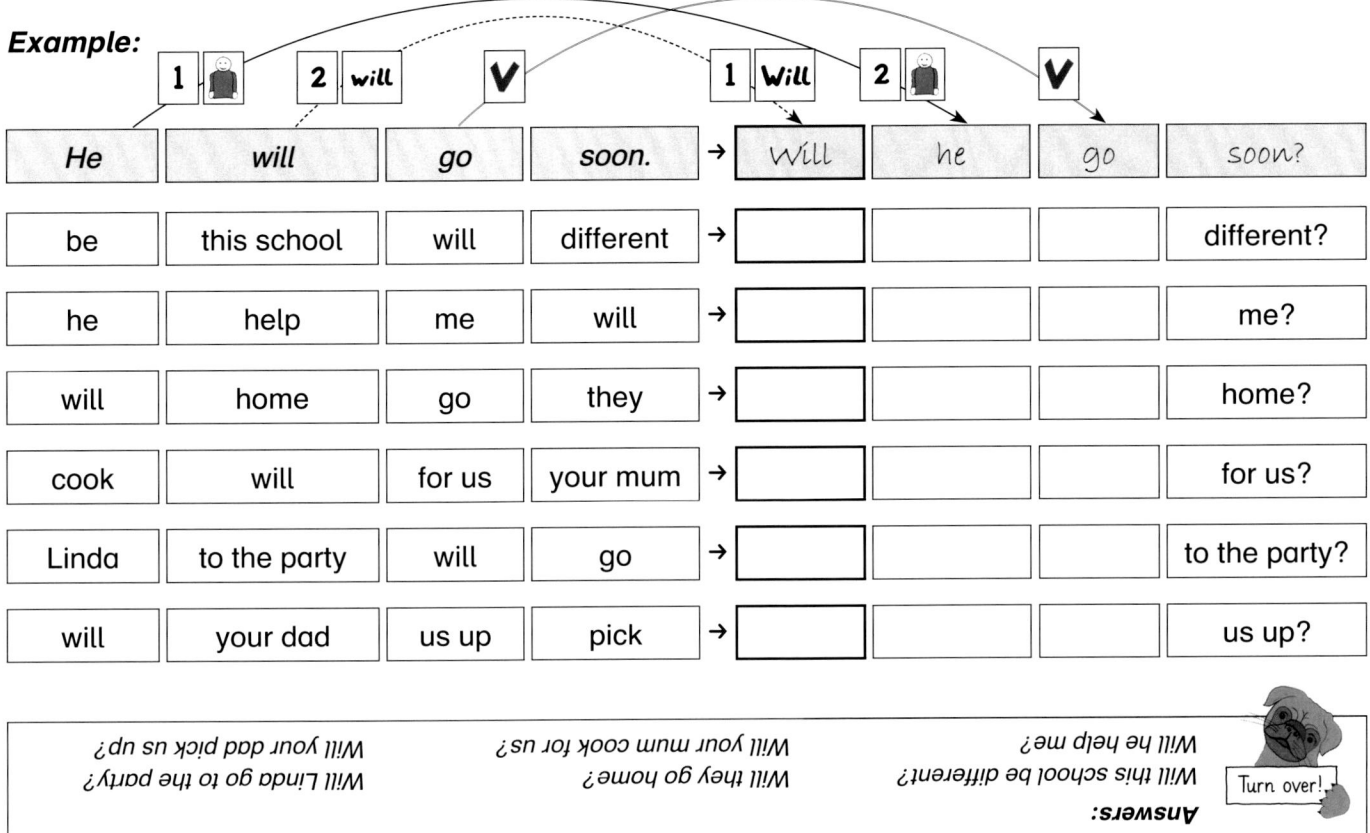

b) Sort the word boxes and form questions with a question word + "will"!

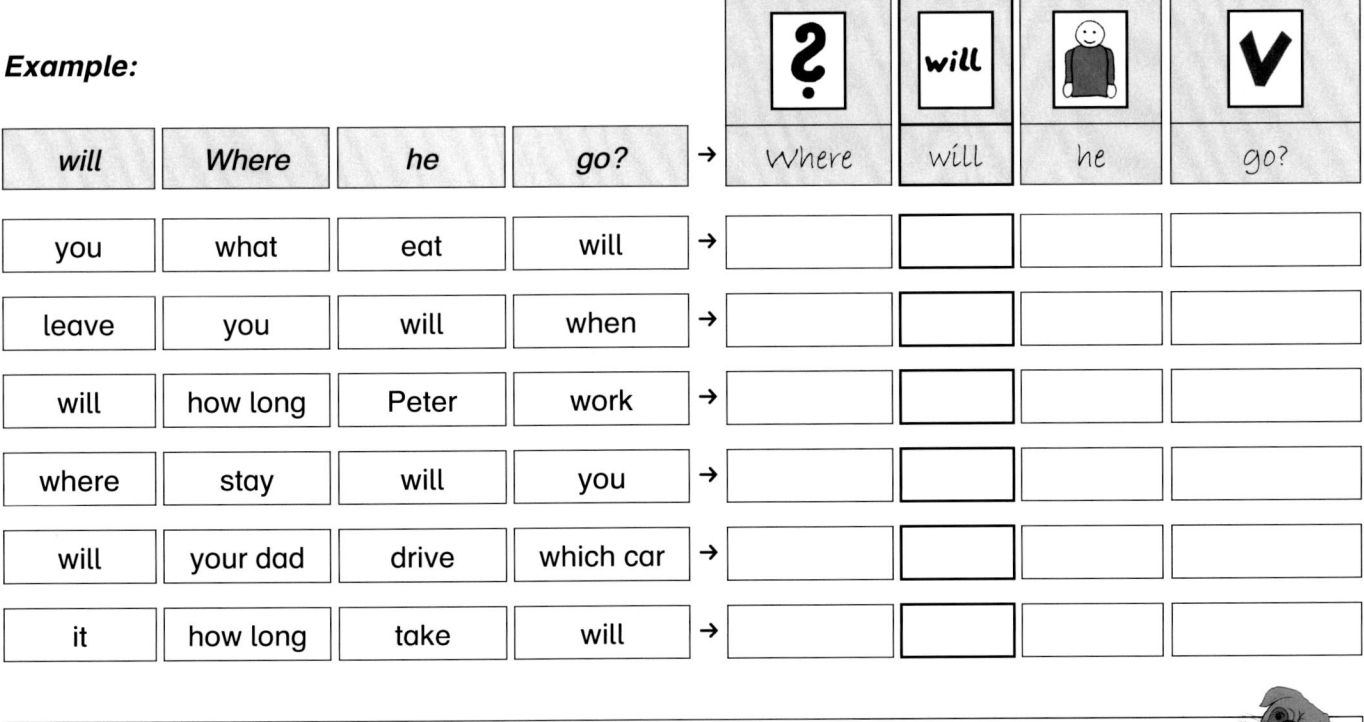

The will-future: Questions with "Will ...?"

a) Sort the word boxes and form questions with "will"!

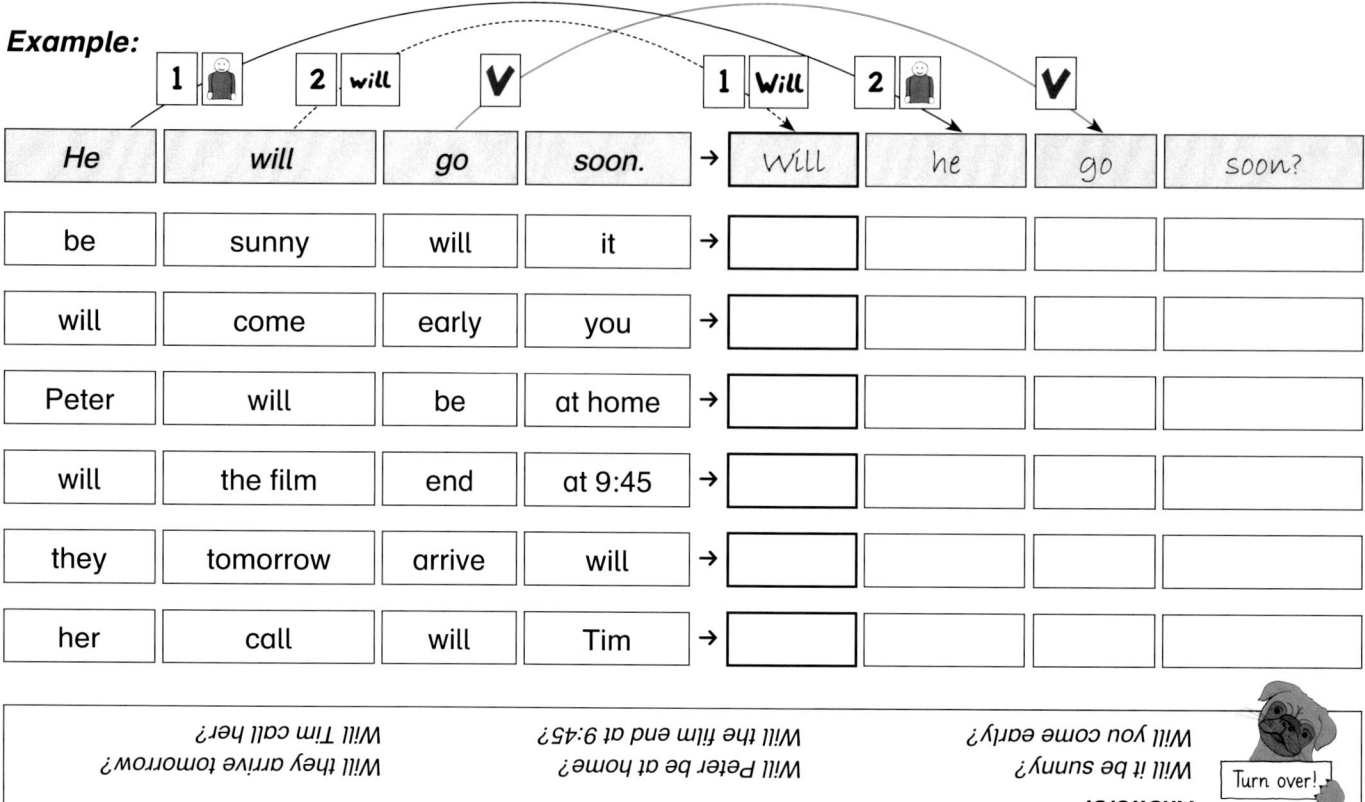

Answers: Will it be sunny? Will you come early? Will Peter be at home? Will the film end at 9:45? Will they arrive tomorrow? Will Tim call her?

b) Form questions using the will-future. Ask for the underlined parts!

Example:	I will go <u>to a tennis match</u> tomorrow.			
Where	will	you	go	tomorrow?
1. Your parents will be back <u>in the evening</u>.				
2. The trip in May will cost <u>€150</u>.				
3. We will get there <u>by train</u>.				
4. Mike will get married <u>in June</u>.				

Answers: When will your parents be back? How much will the trip in May cost? How will we / you get there? When will Mike get married?

The will-future: Short answers – Activity: Tandem

Work with a partner. Fold the paper. One of you is partner A and the other is partner B. Partner A reads the question and partner B gives the short answer with "will" or "won't". Partner A checks the answer. Then partner B reads the sentence and the question and Partner A answers.

Questions: will-future	Short answers: will-future
Partner A	**Partner B**
a) Will we go on a bike tour tomorrow?	We will go on a bike tour tomorrow.
→ Yes, we will.	Yes, we _____.
b) Will John get married in May?	John will get married in June.
→ No he won't. He will get married in June.	No, he _____.
c) Will she go to the zoo next week?	She will go to the cinema next week.
→ No, she won't. She will go to the cinema.	_____.
d) Will the Millers go on holiday next month?	The Millers will go on holiday next month.
→ Yes, they will.	_____.
e) Will the pupils go on a trip next Monday?	The pupils will go on a trip next Friday.
→ No, they won't. They will go on Friday.	_____.
Answers: Questions in the will-future	**Questions in the will-future**
Partner A	**Partner B**
The Smiths will move to Berlin next year.	a) Will the Smiths move to Berlin?
Yes, they _____.	→ Yes, they will.
His father will work in Paris next year.	b) Will his father work in London next year?
No, he _____.	→ No, he won't. He will work in Paris.
Sarah will go to the party tomorrow.	c) Will Sarah go to the party next week?
_____.	→ No, she won't. She will go tomorrow.
The film will end at 8:45.	d) Will the film end at 8:45?
_____.	→ Yes, it will.
We will work on Tuesday.	e) Will we work on Monday?
_____.	→ No, we won't. We will work on Tuesday.

Conditional sentences type I with "will"

> **Beachte:** „will / won't" und „if" – Das präg dir ein! Können **niemals zusammen** sein!

if-clause	main clause with "will"
Simple Present	will + infinitive
If it <u>rains</u>, If it <u>doesn't rain</u>,	I **will stay** at home. I **will go** for a walk.
Bedingung: Wenn es regnet, Wenn es nicht regnet,	(dann) bleibe ich zu Hause. (dann) gehe ich spazieren. : → **Folge**

a) Revision: The will-future

Example:
+ play: He _____ tennis tomorrow.   → He <u>will play</u> tennis tomorrow.

Fold back!				Fold back!
won't arrive	a) – *arrive*: Peter _____ _____ soon.	d) – *have*: We _____ _____ lunch later.		won't have
will help	b) + *help*: Wait, I _____ _____ you!	e) + *visit*: They _____ _____ dad.		will visit
will study	c) + *study*: Jill _____ _____ in Berlin.	f) – *travel*: I _____ _____ a lot.		won't travel

b) Revision: The Simple Present

Example:
+ play: He often _____ tennis.   → He often <u>plays</u> tennis.

Fold back!				Fold back!
sings	a) + *sing*: Sarah always _____ songs.	d) – *be*: He _____ here very often.		isn't
don't meet	b) – *meet*: We _____ _____ very often.	e) + *watch*: I _____ TV every day.		watch
is	c) + *be*: He usually _____ in his room.	f) – *eat*: She _____ _____ a lot.		doesn't eat

c) Conditional sentences: Fill in the will-future for the main clause!

Example: If you <u>go</u> to the zoo,   I <u>will go</u> with you.

		Fold back!
a) If you are late,	you _____ _____ (miss) the bus.	will miss
b) If they don't go to the party,	I _____ _____ (stay) at home, too.	will stay
c) If we don't water the flowers,	our garden _____ _____ (not look) nice.	won't look
d) If you are angry at him,	he _____ _____ (not help) us.	won't help
e) If you run faster,	you _____ _____ (catch) the bus.	will catch
f) If Sarah buys the cola,	I _____ _____ (buy) the pizza.	will buy

Conditional sentences type I with "will"

> Beachte: „will / won't" und „if"
> – Das präg dir ein!
> Können **niemals zusammen** sein!

if-clause	main clause with "will"
Simple Present	will + infinitive
If it <u>rains</u>, If it <u>doesn't rain</u>,	I **will stay** at home. I **will go** for a walk.
Bedingung: Wenn es regnet, Wenn es nicht regnet,	(dann) bleibe ich zu Hause. (dann) gehe ich spazieren. :→ **Folge**

a) The will-future in the main clause

Example: If he <u>feels</u> better later,   he <u>will play</u> tennis.
He <u>will play</u> tennis.   if he <u>feels</u> better.

		Fold back!
a) If the weather stays nice,	we _____ (go) to the park.	will go
b) John _____ (not eat) at a snack bar	if his mother cooks lunch.	won't eat
c) If the film is boring,	I _____ (not watch) the end.	won't watch
d) She _____ (be) happy	if she gets a good mark.	will be

b) The Simple Present in the if-clause

Example: If he <u>feels</u> better later,   he <u>will play</u> tennis.
He <u>will play</u> tennis.   if he <u>feels</u> better.

		Fold back!
a) **If** my friend _____ (not wait) for me,	I will be angry.	doesn't wait
b) Linda will catch the bus	**if** she _____ (hurry).	hurries
c) We will have a big problem	**if** we _____ (not find) the keys!	don't find
d) **If** they _____ (be) too late,	we will still be able to go to the cinema.	aren't

c) Conditional sentences: Fill in the will-future or the Simple Present!

Example: If you <u>go</u> to the zoo,   I <u>will go</u> with you.

		Fold back!
a) If it <u>gets</u> colder,	I _____ (buy) a new winter jacket.	will buy
b) It <u>will be</u> an interesting match	**if** the team _____ (play) well.	plays
c) We <u>will watch</u> TV	**if** Tom _____ (not go) to the party.	doesn't go
d) If Peter <u>doesn't feel</u> better,	he _____ (not come) with us.	won't come
e) If we <u>are</u> late,	the teacher _____ (be) angry.	will be
f) I <u>will help</u> you	**if** I _____ (not be) too busy.	am not

Conditional sentences type I with "will"

> **Beachte:** „will / won't" und „if"
> – Das präg dir ein!
> Können **niemals zusammen** sein!

if-clause	main clause with "will"
Simple Present	will + infinitive
If it <u>rains</u>, If it <u>doesn't rain</u>,	I **will stay** at home. I **will go** for a walk.
Bedingung: Wenn es regnet, Wenn es nicht regnet,	(dann) bleibe ich zu Hause. (dann) gehe ich spazieren. : → **Folge**

Fill in the will-future or the Simple Present!

Example: If you <u>go</u> to the zoo,   I <u>will go</u> with you.

Fold back!

a) **If** it <u>gets</u> hot,	I _____ (go) swimming in the pool.	will go
b) He <u>will move</u> to Berlin	**if** he _____ (find) a job there.	finds
c) They <u>won't wait</u> for us	**if** we _____ (be) late.	are
d) **If** he <u>is</u> at the party,	I _____ (not go) there.	won't go
e) She <u>will be</u> sad	**if** John _____ (not help) her.	doesn't help
f) I <u>will pay</u> for you	**if** you _____ (not have) any money.	don't have
g) **If** you <u>work</u> harder,	you _____ (pass) the test.	will pass
h) **If** he <u>arrives</u> later,	I _____ (not pick) him up.	won't pick
i) We <u>will call</u> Sarah	**if** she _____ (not be) at home.	isn't
j) I <u>will try</u> something different	**if** it _____ (not work).	doesn't work

Adjectives – The comparison of adjectives

a) Add the missing forms "-er" and "-est"!

Adjectives with one syllable			
basic form	comparative -er	superlative -est	
slow			slower – slowest
	shorter		short – shortest
		fastest	fast – faster

b) Fill in the comparison with "adjective-er + than" and "the + adjective-est".

Example: Peter is <u>taller than</u> Jenny. But Tom is <u>the tallest</u>.

1. A frog is _____ _____ a duck. But a worm is _____ _____.
2. The second pencil is _____ _____ the first pencil. But the third pencil is _____ _____.
3. A cyclist is _____ _____ a runner. But the car is _____ _____.

c) Add the missing forms "-er" and "-est"!

Adjectives with two syllables ending with -y → ie			
basic form	comparative -er	superlative -est	
Linda – pretty	Sue	Lynn	prettier – prettiest
Tim	Peter – happier	Phil	happy – happiest
		tiniest	tiny – tinier

d) Fill in the comparison with "adjective-er + than" and "the + adjective-est".

Example: Peter is <u>taller than</u> Jenny. But Tom is <u>the tallest</u>.

1. Sue is _____ _____ Linda. But Lynn is _____ _____.
2. Peter is _____ _____ Tim. But Phil is _____ _____.
3. A butterfly is _____ _____ a mouse. But the worm is _____ _____.

e) Add the missing forms with "more" and "most"!

Adjectives with more than one syllable			
basic form	comparative more	superlative most	
expensive			more expensive – most expensive
		most difficult	difficult – more difficult
Linda	Sue – more beautiful	Lynn	beautiful – most beautiful

f) Fill in the comparison with "more + adjective + than" and "the most + adjective".

Example: History is <u>more interesting than</u> Maths. But English is <u>the most interesting</u> subject.

1. The second dress is _____ _____ _____ the first. But the third dress is _____ _____ _____.
2. English homework is _____ _____ _____ German homework. But Maths is _____ _____ _____.
3. Sue is _____ _____ _____ Linda. But Lynn is _____ _____ _____.

b) ... slower than ... the slowest / ... shorter than ... the shortest / ... faster than ... the fastest
d) ... prettier than ... the prettiest / ... happier than ... the happiest / ... tinier than ... the tiniest
f) ... more expensive than ... the most expensive / ... more difficult than ... the most difficult / ... more beautiful ... the most beautiful

Adjectives – The comparison of adjectives

a) Add the missing forms!

Adjectives with one syllable			
basic form	comparative -er	superlative -est	
high			higher – highest
big			bigger – biggest
Paul nice	Adrian	Marc	nicer – nicest

Adjectives with two syllables ending with -y → ie			
basic form	comparative -er	superlative -est	
Linda pretty	Sue	Lynn	prettier – prettiest
Dave angry	Lisa	Peter	angrier – angriest
dirty			dirtier – dirtiest

Adjectives with more than one syllable			
basic form	comparative more	superlative most	
expensive			more expensive – most expensive
difficult			more difficult – most difficult
Linda beautiful	Sue	Lynn	more beautiful – most beautiful

Adjectives with special forms			
basic form	comparative	superlative	
good			better – best
bad			worse – worst
many			more – many

b) Fill in the correct form!

tired: My mum is _____ _____ than my father.   more tired

happy: I am _____ _____ person in the world.   the happiest

bad: He is _____ than my sister at Maths.   worse

famous: This man is _____ _____ than anybody else.   more famous

long: This street is really _____. It is _____ _____ street I have ever seen.   long – the longest

hot: It's _____ inside than outside of the house.   hotter

funny: This comic is _____ than the one in the magazine.   funnier

many: You can see _____ sights in London – _____ than in Stuttgart.   many – more

fast: I am _____ than my sister but my brother is _____ _____.   faster – fastest

Adjectives – The comparison of adjectives

a) Add the missing forms!

Adjectives with one syllable			
basic form	comparative -er	superlative -est	Fold back!
strong			stronger – strongest
hot			hotter – hottest
large			larger – largest

Adjectives with two syllables ending with -y → ie			
basic form	comparative -er	superlative -est	Fold back!
heavy			heavier – heaviest
dirty			dirtier – dirtiest

Adjectives with two syllables ending with -le / -er			
basic form	comparative -er	superlative -est	Fold back!
simple			simpler – simplest
clever			cleverer – cleverest

Adjectives with more than one syllable			
basic form	comparative more	superlative most	Fold back!
popular			more popular – most popular
important			more important – most important

Adjectives with special forms			
basic form	comparative	superlative	Fold back!
good			better – best
bad			worse – worst
many			more – many

b) Fill in the correct form!

careful: You must be _____ _____ with the glasses! — more careful

easy: This is ____ _____ exercise I have ever done! — the easiest

bad: This game is _____ _____ the other! — worse than

interesting: What an _____ book! — interesting

small: The old dress is _____ _____ the new dress. — smaller than

thin: Wow, you have become _____. You are _____ _____ last year. — thin / thinner – thinner than

noisy: This is ____ _____ town I have ever been to! — the noisiest

good: Today was a _____ day and tomorrow will be even _____! — good – better

colourful: How _____! This is ___ _____ _____ shirt I have ever seen! — colourful – the most colourful

Past Progressive – Positive statements

Du verwendest das Past Progressive, um zu betonen, dass **etwas in der Vergangenheit länger andauerte**.

I / You / He ...   was / were   +   verb-ing

Example: We _____ + _____ football all afternoon.
- ○ was playing
- ● were playing

a) I _____ a book.
- ○ was reading (W)
- ○ were reading (e)
- ○ was eating (g)
- ○ were eating (o)

b) Peter and Tim _____ TV.
- ○ was watching (o)
- ○ were watching (e)
- ○ was reading (d)
- ○ are reading (g)

c) You _____ some friends.
- ○ was visiting (e)
- ○ were visiting (l)
- ○ was talking (d)
- ○ were talking (g)

d) The pig _____ an apple.
- ○ were eating (e)
- ○ was eating (l)
- ○ were drinking (d)
- ○ was drinking (w)

e) Mr Smith _____ a car.
- ○ were driving (l)
- ○ was driving (d)
- ○ was riding (e)
- ○ were riding (w)

f) They _____ tea.
- ○ was eating (e)
- ○ was drinking (d)
- ○ were eating (w)
- ○ were drinking (o)

g) Paul _____ a letter.
- ○ was going (e)
- ○ were going (o)
- ○ was writing (n)
- ○ were writing (d)

h) She _____ fun.
- ○ was wearing (w)
- ○ was having (e)
- ○ was taking (o)
- ○ were having (d)

Write down the letter behind each answer. Keep to the order a, b, c ...
If your answers are correct you can read your code:
___ ___ ___ ___   ___ ___ ___ ___ !

Now you! Put the verb into the Past Progressive!

a) clean: I _____ _____ my room.   was cleaning

b) work: They _____ _____ in the garden.   were working

c) paint: Sarah _____ _____ a picture.   was painting

d) play: My friends _____ _____ games.   were playing

e) sleep: Peter _____ _____ in his bed.   was sleeping

f) look: We _____ _____ for my keys.   were looking

g) wait: I _____ _____ for you at the bus stop.   was waiting

Fold back!

Past Progressive – Positive statements

Du verwendest das Past Progressive, um zu betonen, dass **etwas in der Vergangenheit länger andauerte.**

Form positive statements!

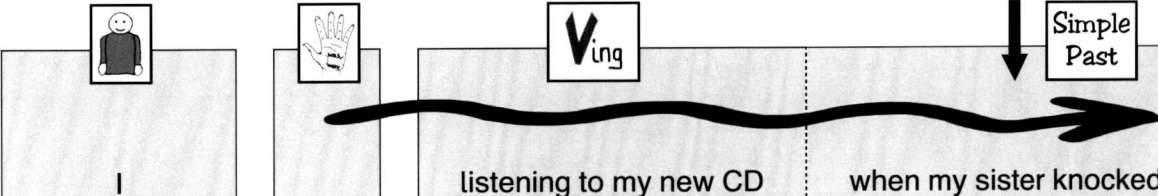

		V_{ing}	Simple Past
I		listening to my new CD	when my sister knocked at my door.
You		repairing your bike	when I called you.
Mr Smith		working in the garden	when the postman came.
Linda	was	reading her book	when her mother called her.
The dog	were	playing in the garden	when the cat jumped into the garden.
We		walking in the park	when it suddenly started to rain.
They		watching TV	when the dog jumped on the sofa.
My father		having a shower	when the phone rang.
Peter and I		were dancing	when the lights went out.
~~My friends~~		~~planning a party~~	~~when I came in.~~

Example:

My friends   were   planning a party   when I came in.

1. _____
2. _____
3. _____
4. _____
5. _____
6. _____
7. _____
8. _____
9. _____

Answers:
1. I was listening to my new CD when my sister knocked at my door.
2. You were repairing your bike when I called you.
3. Mr Smith was working in the garden when the postman came.
4. Linda was reading her book when her mother called her.
5. The dog was playing in the garden when the cat jumped into the garden.
6. We were walking in the park when it suddenly started to rain.
7. They were watching TV when the dog jumped on the sofa.
8. My father was having a shower when the phone rang.
9. Peter and I were dancing when the lights went out.

Turn over!

Past Progressive – Positive statements

			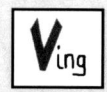	
	I / You / He ...	was / were	+ verb-ing	
Example:	I	was	playing	football.
	They	were	playing	football.

Du verwendest das Past Progressive, um zu betonen, dass etwas in der Vergangenheit länger andauerte.

Use the correct verb from the verb box and put the verb into the Past Progressive!

1. My mother _____ _____ dinner when the cat jumped on the table.
2. The cats _____ _____ milk when the dog came into the kitchen.
3. Peter _____ _____ to the radio when Sarah opened his door.
4. My parents _____ _____ TV when I came in.
5. I _____ _____ a book when my sister came in.
6. We _____ _____ our homework when the bell rang.
7. I _____ _____ for you when the bus arrived.
8. They _____ _____ at her when she started to cry.
9. Linda _____ _____ her hair when the phone rang.
10. They _____ _____ for a test when the fire alarm went on.
11. We _____ _____ football when Tom suddenly fell down.
12. Tom and Sue _____ _____ in the park when it started to rain.
13. My father _____ _____ on the sofa when the dog jumped on him.
14. My friends _____ _____ me with the sandwiches when my mother came in.

when she called me → Simple Past
I was playing football ↝ Past Progressive

| study | drink | listen | wash | do | cook | play |
| wait | read | laugh | watch | sleep | walk | help |

Answers:
1. My mother was cooking ...
2. The cats were drinking ...
3. Peter was listening ...
4. My parents were watching ...
5. I was reading ...
6. We were doing ...
7. I was waiting ...
8. They were laughing ...
9. Linda was washing ...
10. They were studying ...
11. We were playing ...
12. Tom and Sue were walking ...
13. My father was sleeping ...
14. My friends were helping ...

Turn over!

Past Progressive – Spelling

a) after a short stressed vowel at the end	→			double the consonant
	r<u>u</u>n	nn	ru**nn**ing	
b) "e" at the end	→			leave out the "e"
	lov<u>e</u>	ℯ	loving	
c) "ie" at the end	→			change "ie" to "y"
	d<u>ie</u>	y	d**y**ing	
d) verb ending with "l"	→			double the "l"
	trave<u>l</u>	ll	trave**ll**ing	

Sort the verbs from the box below. Which spelling category is correct when adding "-ing"?

g<u>e</u>t – smil<u>e</u> – sw<u>i</u>m – l<u>ie</u> – sw<u>a</u>p – rid<u>e</u> – pl<u>a</u>n – mak<u>e</u> – mod<u>e</u>l – s<u>i</u>t – cancel – mov<u>e</u> – p<u>u</u>t – t<u>ie</u> – tak<u>e</u>

double consonant	ℯ	ie → y	l → ll
r<u>u</u>n → running	write → writing	die → dying	travel → travelling

Answers: 1.: getting – swimming – swapping – planning – sitting – putting **2.:** smiling – riding – making – driving – moving – taking **3.:** lying – tying **4.:** modelling – cancelling

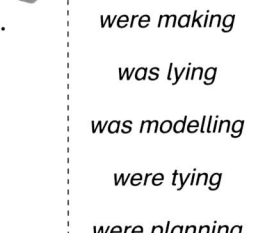

Fill in the Past Progressive. Be careful with the spelling!

1. make: We _____ _____ a cake when my mother came into the kitchen. — *were making*
2. lie: The cow _____ _____ in the grass when we came to the farm. — *was lying*
3. model: She _____ _____ when she suddenly fell. — *was modelling*
4. tie: They _____ _____ the ropes when the storm began. — *were tying*
5. plan: My parents _____ _____ our next trip when the phone rang. — *were planning*
6. have: Look! Sarah _____ _____ breakfast when her cat jumped on the table. — *was having*
7. write: The teacher _____ _____ on the board when Tom opened the door. — *was writing*

Can you guess the right verb? Put it into the Past Progressive!

1. She _____ _____ a letter when her friend called. — *was writing*
2. My father _____ _____ the car when the accident happened. — *was driving*
3. We _____ _____ in the sea when a ship passed us. — *were swimming*
4. Peter _____ _____ his bike when it started to rain. — *was riding*
5. We _____ _____ for the bus when I suddenly fell. — *were running*
6. They _____ _____ on the sofa when the dog jumped on it. — *were sitting*

Past Progressive – Negative statements (long form) with "was not / were not"

	I / You / He ...	was / were	not	+	verb-ing
Example:	I	was	not		singing.
	They	were	not		singing.

Form negative statements!

Example: I was * singing a song. → I was not singing a song.

1. We were * waiting for him. → _____
2. My parents were * going home. → _____
3. My friend was * reading a book. → _____
4. Our cat was * drinking milk. → _____
5. The children were * having lunch. → _____
6. My sister was * helping me. → _____
7. I was * sitting on my bed. → _____
8. They were * working hard. → _____
9. He was * sleeping on the sofa. → _____
10. My friends were * watching TV. → _____
11. I was * playing the piano. → _____
12. We were * swimming in the sea. → _____
13. Lynn was * driving the car. → _____
14. The Millers were * travelling. → _____
15. Peter was * listening to him. → _____
16. We were * playing in the park. → _____

Answers:
1. We were not waiting for him.
2. My parents were not going home.
3. My friend was not reading a book.
4. Our cat was not drinking milk.
5. The children were not having lunch.
6. My sister was not helping me.
7. I was not sitting on my bed.
8. They were not working hard.
9. He was not sleeping on the sofa.
10. My friends were not watching TV.
11. I was not playing the piano.
12. We were not swimming in the sea.
13. Lynn was not driving the car.
14. The Millers were not travelling.
15. Peter was not listening to him.
16. We were not playing in the park.

Past Progressive – Negative statements (long form) with "was not / were not"

Form negative statements!

Example: I was singing a song. → I was <u>not</u> singing a song.
They were sleeping. → They were <u>not</u> sleeping.

👤	✋	not	V_{ing}	↓ Simple Past
I The ice My friends My father She They We My mother The pupils Tom	was were	**not**	reading my book melting running around driving the car eating walking in the park swimming in the sea cooking in the kitchen taking a test dancing	when you phoned. when we fell on it. when the teacher came in. when the accident happened. when she talked to you on the phone. when it started to rain. when the storm began. when the fire broke out. when the headmaster came in. when the lights went out at the disco.

1. _____
2. _____
3. _____
4. _____
5. _____
6. _____
7. _____
8. _____
9. _____
10. _____

Answers:
1. I was not reading my book …
2. The ice was not melting …
3. My friends were not running around …
4. My father was not driving the car …
5. She was not eating …
6. They were not walking in the park …
7. We were not swimming in the sea …
8. My mother was not cooking …
9. The pupils were not taking a test …
10. Tom was not dancing …

Turn over!

Past Progressive – Negative statements (long form) with "was not / were not"

Form negative statements!

Example: buy: I <u>was not reading</u> a book when you phoned.
repair: We <u>were not repairing</u> the car when my father arrived.

1. take: They _____ _____ _____ an English test when the headmaster came in.
2. eat: We _____ _____ _____ a pizza when my mother called us for dinner.
3. clean: My mother _____ _____ _____ the kitchen when the dog ran through.
4. drive: I _____ _____ _____ the car when the accident happened.
5. read: Tom _____ _____ _____ a comic when his friend came for a visit.
6. watch: We _____ _____ _____ a DVD when my sister began to study.
7. wait: They _____ _____ _____ at the bus stop when the bus arrived.
8. dance: My friends and I _____ _____ _____ when I suddenly fell.
9. ride: She _____ _____ _____ her bike when it started to snow.
10. work: I _____ _____ _____ in the garage when I saw a mouse.
11. have: My parents _____ _____ _____ breakfast when the cat jumped onto the table.
12. wash: My mum _____ _____ _____ my shirt when the water stopped running.
13. take: Peter _____ _____ _____ the dog for a walk when it started to rain.
14. talk: Tom and John _____ _____ _____ to Linda when my mother met them.
15. run: The pupils _____ _____ _____ around when the teacher came in.
16. sleep: I _____ _____ _____ when my friend rang the bell.

Answers:
1. They were not taking …
2. We were not eating …
3. My mother was not cleaning …
4. I was not driving …
5. Tom was not reading …
6. We were not watching …
7. They were not waiting …
8. My friends and I were not dancing …
9. She was not riding …
10. I was not working …
11. My parents were not having …
12. My mum was not washing …
13. Peter was not taking …
14. Tom and John were not talking …
15. The pupils were not running …
16. I was not sleeping …

Past Progressive – Negative statements (short form) with "wasn't / weren't"

Form negative statements using the short form!

	wasn't / weren't	Ving	
I		working on my project	when you called.
My father		painting the fence	when it started to rain.
It		raining	when I came outside.
Peter		walking in the park	when it started to snow.
We		listening to music	when my father came in.
My parents	wasn't	having lunch	when the cat stole a fish.
They	weren't	swimming in the lake	when the storm began.
The children		running around	when their teacher came in.
My mother		cooking for dinner	when I came home.
My friends		waiting at the bus stop	when the bus arrived.
The dog		playing in the garden	when the postman came.
The pupils		writing	when the headmaster came in.

Example: I   <u>wasn't</u>   <u>reading</u> a book   when you phoned.
We   <u>weren't</u>   <u>repairing</u> the car   when my father arrived.

1. _____
2. _____
3. _____
4. _____
5. _____
6. _____
7. _____
8. _____
9. _____
10. _____
11. _____
12. _____

Answers:
1. I wasn't working …
2. My father wasn't painting …
3. It wasn't raining …
4. Peter wasn't walking …
5. We weren't listening …
6. My parents weren't having lunch …
7. They weren't swimming …
8. The children weren't running …
9. My mother wasn't cooking …
10. My friends weren't waiting …
11. The dog wasn't playing …
12. The pupils weren't writing …

Past Progressive – Negative statements (short form) with "wasn't / weren't"

Example:

Long form:	I	was ~~n't~~ not	playing	football.
Short form:	I	wasn't	playing	football.
Long form:	You	were ~~n't~~ not	playing	football.
Short form:	You	weren't	playing	football.

Rewrite the sentences using the short form!

1. I *was not* reading a book. → _____
2. He *was not* working in the garden. → _____
3. My friends *were not* going home. → _____
4. They *were not* planning the trip. → _____
5. Sarah *was not* cleaning her room. → _____
6. My parents *were not* driving home. → _____
7. I *was not* listening to him. → _____
8. She *was not* dancing. → _____
9. We *were not* swimming in the river. → _____
10. The cat *was not* drinking our milk. → _____
11. Peter *was not* working. → _____
12. I *was not* listening to the music. → _____
13. My friends *were not* running around. → _____
14. The dog *was not* playing in the park. → _____

Answers:

1. *I wasn't reading a book.*
2. *He wasn't working in the garden.*
3. *My friends weren't going home.*
4. *They weren't planning the trip.*
5. *Sarah wasn't cleaning her room.*
6. *My parents weren't driving home.*
7. *I wasn't listening to him.*
8. *She wasn't dancing.*
9. *We weren't swimming in the river.*
10. *The cat wasn't drinking our milk.*
11. *Peter wasn't working.*
12. *I wasn't listening to the music.*
13. *My friends weren't running around.*
14. *The dog wasn't playing in the park.*

Past Progressive – Negative Statements (short form) with "wasn't / weren't"

Form negative statements! Use the short form!

Example: I <u>wasn't playing football</u> when it started to rain.
We <u>weren't repairing</u> the bike when my father came into the garage.

1. take: We _____ _____ a test when the head teacher came in.

2. prepare: I _____ _____ dinner when the bell rang.

3. talk: She _____ _____ to her classmate when the teacher looked at her.

4. sleep: He _____ _____ on the sofa when his parents came home.

5. clean: My mother _____ _____ the kitchen when her friend phoned.

6. wait: We _____ _____ at the bus stop when the bus arrived.

7. play: They _____ _____ in the garden when it started to rain.

8. listen: He _____ _____ to the teacher when the teacher talked to him.

9. plan: They _____ _____ a bike tour when we arrived.

10. cross: My friend _____ _____ the street when a car showed up.

11. close: Tim _____ _____ the door when the door glass broke.

12. rain: It _____ _____ when we went outside.

13. play: We _____ _____ in our room when Linda suddenly screamed.

14. sit: The dog _____ _____ on the sofa when I came into the living room.

15. have: They _____ _____ dinner when the guests arrived.

16. work: He _____ _____ on the project when his friend called.

Answers:

1. We weren't taking …
2. I wasn't preparing …
3. She wasn't talking …
4. He wasn't sleeping …
5. My mother wasn't cleaning …
6. We weren't waiting …
7. They weren't playing …
8. He wasn't listening …
9. They weren't planning …
10. My friend wasn't crossing …
11. Tim wasn't closing …
12. It wasn't raining …
13. We weren't playing …
14. The dog wasn't sitting …
15. They weren't having dinner …
16. He wasn't working …

Turn over!

Past Progressive – Questions with "Was …?" / "Were …?"

Form questions to ask what these people were doing in the past.

| Was / Were | you / Linda / Peter / my friends / Mrs Carter / Jim and Tom / the cat / they / my mother / the Millers / it / the pupils | watching / cleaning / talking / eating / driving / playing / drinking / waiting / cooking / swimming / raining / doing | TV? / her room? / to his teacher? / a pizza? / to the city centre? / football? / milk? / for Peter? / dinner? / in their pool? / all afternoon? / their homework? |

Example:

   Were   you   going   home?

1. ___
2. ___
3. ___
4. ___
5. ___
6. ___
7. ___
8. ___
9. ___
10. ___
11. ___
12. ___

Answers:

1. Were you watching TV?
2. Was Linda cleaning her room?
3. Was Peter talking to his teacher?
4. Were my friends eating a pizza?
5. Was Mrs Carter driving to the city centre?
6. Were Jim and Tom playing football?
7. Was the cat drinking milk?
8. Were they waiting for Peter?
9. Was my mother cooking dinner?
10. Were the Millers swimming in their pool?
11. Was it raining all afternoon?
12. Were the pupils doing their homework?

Past Progressive – Questions with "Was ...?" / "Were ...?"

Form questions to ask what these people were doing in the past.

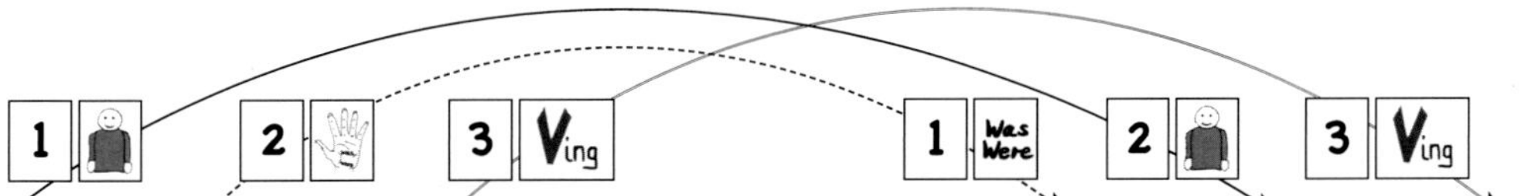

They	were	singing	a song.	→	Were	they	singing	a song?
He	was	playing	football.	→	Was	he	playing	football?

Tim	was	reading	a book.	→				
We	were	going	home.	→				
You	were	riding	a bike.	→				
Dad	was	repairing	the car.	→				
Lynn	was	working	hard.	→				
They	were	talking	a lot.	→				
You	were	helping	her.	→				
Jane	was	eating	lunch.	→				
They	were	cleaning	the house.	→				
She	was	writing	a letter.	→				
You	were	watching	TV.	→				
He	was	playing	tennis.	→				

Answers:
1. Was Tim reading a book?
2. Were we going home?
3. Were you riding a bike?
4. Was dad repairing the car?
5. Was Lynn working hard?
6. Were they talking a lot?
7. Were you helping her?
8. Was Jane eating lunch?
9. Were they cleaning the house?
10. Was she writing a letter?
11. Were you watching TV?
12. Was he playing tennis?

Turn over!

Past Progressive – Questions with "Was ...?" / "Were ...?"

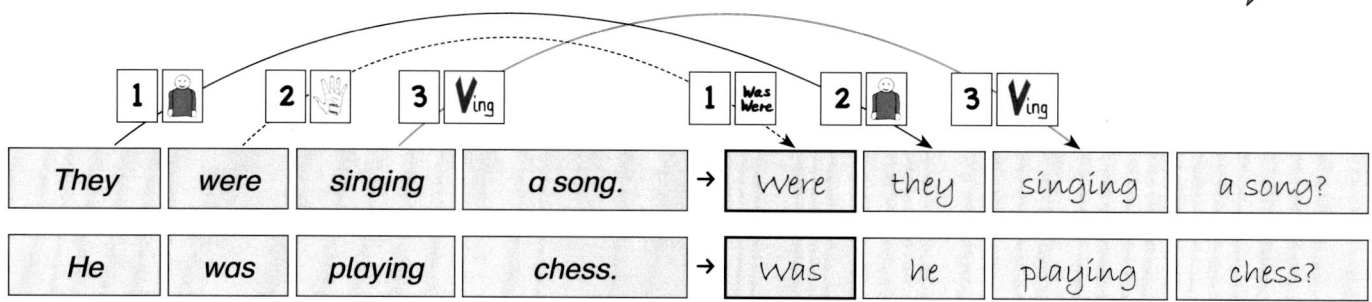

Form questions! Look at the pictures and ask what these people were doing!

Example: Was he closing the door? — he – close – the door

1. _____ — she – dance
2. _____ — he – clean – his room
3. _____ — they – play – football
4. _____ — you – ride – your bike
5. _____ — they – talk
6. _____ — you – listen – to music
7. _____ — she – sleep
8. _____ — you – laugh – at me
9. _____ — she – clean – the board
10. _____ — he – write – a letter

Answers:
1. Was she dancing?
2. Was he cleaning his room?
3. Were they playing football?
4. Were you riding your bike?
5. Were they talking?
6. Were you listening to music?
7. Was she sleeping?
8. Were you laughing at me?
9. Was she cleaning the board?
10. Was he writing a letter?

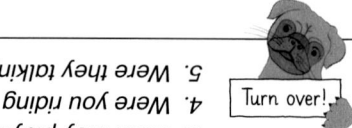

Past Progressive – Questions with question words

Find the correct order!
Form questions to ask what these people were doing in the past.

Example:

were	staying	Where	you	→ Where	were	you	staying?
Why	running	was	he	→ Why	was	he	running?
were	Where	going	you	→			
How long	Peter	sleeping	was	→			
driving	Which car	were	you	→			
was	she	doing	What	→			
Where	walking	Linda	was	→			
you	Whose cap	wearing	were	→			
was	he	What	playing	→			
they	Where	running	were	→			
was	the band	Which songs	playing	→			
Peter	Whose bike	riding	was	→			

Answers:
1. Where were you going?
2. How long was Peter sleeping?
3. Which car were you driving?
4. What was she doing?
5. Where was Linda walking?
6. Whose cap were you wearing?
7. What was he playing?
8. Where were they running?
9. Which songs was the band playing?
10. Whose bike was Peter riding?

Turn over!

Past Progressive – Questions with question words

Form questions to ask what these people were doing in the past.

Where	were you	playing	football?
How long	was he	sleeping	on the sofa?
What	were they	doing	in my room?
Who	was my mother	talking	to at school?
Whose dog	was Linda	taking	for a walk?
Which bike	was your father	repairing	in the garage?
How long	were your parents	driving	to the city centre?
Why	were you	sleeping	all day?
Where	was she	waiting	for him?
What	was he	searching	for?

Example:

Why ____ were you ____ phoning ____ all afternoon?

1. _____
2. _____
3. _____
4. _____
5. _____
6. _____
7. _____
8. _____
9. _____
10. _____

Answers:

1. Where were you playing football?
2. How long was he sleeping on the sofa?
3. What were they doing in my room?
4. Who was my mother talking to at school?
5. Whose dog was Linda taking for a walk?
6. Which bike was your father repairing in the garage?
7. How long were your parents driving to the city centre?
8. Why were you sleeping all day?
9. Where was she waiting for him?
10. What was he searching for?

Past Progressive – Questions with question words

Ask for the underlined parts.

Example: Where were you going to?
I was going <u>to school</u> when my mother phoned me.

> **Vergiss nicht:** <u>Präpositionen</u> wie:
> to / at / for / with …
> werden in der Frage aufgenommen!
> Who are you talking <u>to</u>?
> What is he looking <u>at</u>?
> What are you waiting <u>for</u>?

1. _____
   She was singing *in* her room all day long.

2. _____
   I was cleaning the kitchen yesterday morning.

3. _____
   Linda was wearing Peter's jacket all evening.

4. _____
   Your mother was searching *for* the green shirt yesterday afternoon.

5. _____
   We were waiting *at* the bus stop at 5 o'clock yesterday.

6. _____
   Yesterday morning Peter was waiting for Tina because it was her birthday.

7. _____
   His father was repairing my bike at 6 o'clock yesterday.

8. _____
   They were looking *for* a present all afternoon.

9. _____
   Sarah was going for a walk *at* 4 o'clock.

10. _____
    Tom and Peter were making the cake *for* Tina.

Answers:

1. Where was she singing all day long?
2. What were you cleaning yesterday morning? (Nicht: What was I … ← In der Regel fragt man sich selbst nicht, was man tut.)
3. Whose jacket was Linda wearing all evening?
4. Which shirt was your mother searching for yesterday afternoon?
5. Where were you waiting at 5 o'clock yesterday? (Nicht: What were we … ← In der Regel fragt man sich selbst nicht, was man tut.)
6. Why was Peter waiting for Tina yesterday morning?
7. What was his father repairing at 6 o'clock yesterday?
8. What were they looking for all afternoon?
9. When was Sarah going for a walk?
10. Who were Tom and Peter making the cake for?

Turn over!

Simple Past and Past Progressive

a) Can you remember how to form the Simple Past with regular verbs?
   Say what these people did or didn't do yesterday.

Example: ⊕ I _____ (work) a lot yesterday.
I <u>worked</u> a lot yesterday.

⊖ I _____ (not / work) yesterday.
I <u>didn't work</u> yesterday.

Fold back!	⊕ Positive statements with verb-ed	⊖ Negative statements with didn't	Fold back!
repaired	a) He _____ (repair) his bike.	g) Peter and Tim _____ (not / play) tennis.	didn't play
cleaned	b) I _____ (clean) my room.	h) She _____ (not / work).	didn't work
played	c) They _____ (play) football.	i) They _____ (not / wait) for me.	didn't wait
helped	d) Linda _____ (help) her mum.	j) I _____ (not / cook) dinner.	didn't cook
danced	e) We _____ (dance) at the disco.	k) Paul _____ (not / wash) his hair.	didn't wash
painted	f) She _____ (paint) her room.	l) They _____ (not / open) the door.	didn't open

b) Can you remember how to form the Simple Past with irregular verbs?
   Say what these people did or didn't do yesterday.

Example: ⊕ I _____ (eat) lunch yesterday.
I <u>ate</u> lunch yesterday.

⊖ I _____ (not / eat) lunch yesterday.
I <u>didn't eat</u> lunch yesterday.

Fold back!	⊕ Positive statements	⊖ Negative statements	Fold back!
wrote	a) She _____ (write) a letter.	g) Lynn and Tim _____ (not / go) home.	didn't go
bought	b) I _____ (buy) a new CD.	h) He _____ (not / forget) about it.	didn't forget
ran	c) We _____ (run) to school.	i) We _____ (not / know) her.	didn't know
came	d) Tom _____ (come) home.	j) I _____ (not / break) the vase.	didn't break
had	e) They _____ (have) breakfast.	k) Sarah _____ (not / find) the key.	didn't find
gave	f) He _____ (give) me the book.	l) They _____ (not / eat) pizza for lunch.	didn't eat

Simple Past and Past Progressive

a) Can you remember how to form the Simple Past with regular verbs?
Say what these people did or didn't do yesterday. Choose a verb from the verb box.

Example: ⊕ I _____ tennis yesterday. I <u>played</u> tennis yesterday.
⊖ I _____ tennis yesterday. I <u>didn't play</u> tennis yesterday.

wash – listen – visit – play – clean – watch – repair – work – call – cook – rain – wait

Fold back!			Fold back!
repaired	a) +: He _____ his bike.	g) +: Jenny _____ her friend.	called
cooked	b) +: I _____ dinner.	h) –: He _____ to the teacher.	didn't listen
didn't wait	c) –: They _____ for Peter.	i) –: Tim and Pit _____ on their project.	didn't work
didn't play	d) –: Joe _____ tennis.	j) +: I _____ the car.	washed
rained	e) +: It _____ a lot.	k) –: Sue _____ her room.	didn't clean
didn't watch	f) –: I _____ TV.	l) +: We _____ our grandma.	visited

b) Can you remember how to form the Simple Past with irregular verbs?
Say what these people did or didn't do yesterday. Choose a verb from the verb box.

Example: ⊕ I _____ lunch yesterday. I <u>ate</u> tennis yesterday.
⊖ I _____ lunch yesterday. I <u>didn't play</u> tennis yesterday.

have – buy – sleep – teach – eat – read – ride – take – catch – write – sell – go – see – be

Fold back!			Fold back!
caught	a) +: Tim _____ a mouse.	h) +: Toby _____ his new bike.	rode
had	b) +: We _____ dinner.	i) +: She _____ him Maths.	taught
didn't write	c) –: They _____ a postcard.	j) –: Sue and Pit _____ the bus home.	didn't take
didn't read	d) –: Sue _____ my book.	k) +: I _____ pizza for dinner.	ate
bought	e) +: We _____ many CDs.	l) –: Joe _____ his bike.	didn't sell
didn't sleep	f) –: I _____ a lot.	m) +: We _____ to the cinema.	went
saw	g) +: He _____ bears at the zoo.	n) +: I _____ at home.	was

Simple Past and Past Progressive

a) Can you remember how to form the Simple Past with regular verbs?
   Say what these people did or didn't do yesterday. Choose a verb that fits!

Example: +: I _____ my room yesterday. → ⊕ I <u>cleaned</u> my room yesterday.
−: I _____ my room yesterday. → ⊖ I <u>didn't clean</u> my room yesterday.

listened	a) +: They _____ to the new CD.	g) +: Paula _____ for the bus.	waited
closed	b) +: It was cold. She _____ the window.	h) −: He _____ tennis with his friend.	didn't play
didn't play	c) −: We _____ football in the garden.	i) +: Tom and Peter _____ TV.	watched
asked	d) +: The teacher _____ a lot of questions.	j) +: I _____ at the disco.	danced
didn't laugh	e) −: I _____ at Tom's jokes. They were boring.	k) +: The room was dirty. They _____ it.	cleaned
didn't play	f) −: He _____ the drums.	l) −: Linda _____ my questions.	didn't answer

b) Can you remember how to form the Simple Past with irregular verbs?
   Say what these people did or didn't do yesterday. Choose a verb that fits!

Example: +: I _____ lunch yesterday. → ⊕ I <u>ate</u> lunch yesterday.
−: I _____ lunch yesterday. → ⊖ I <u>didn't eat</u> lunch yesterday.

had	a) +: We _____ breakfast in the morning.	g) −: Paul _____ any songs with us.	didn't sing
was	b) +: It _____ my brother's birthday.	h) −: He _____ to school by bus.	didn't go
took	c) +: They _____ a lot of photos at the zoo.	i) −: Tom and Peter _____ an article for the newspaper.	didn't write
didn't do	d) −: Peter _____ his homework.	j) +: I _____ some sugar at the supermarket.	bought
rode	e) +: I _____ my new bike.	k) −: Linda _____ a lot of water.	didn't drink
didn't eat	f) −: We _____ lunch at the restaurant.	l) +: They _____ to the cinema.	went

Simple Past and Past Progressive

a) I was reading a book
while
my brother was watching TV.

> Das Past Progressive verwendest du auch um auszudrücken, dass in der Vergangenheit **zwei Handlungen zur gleichen Zeit** abliefen.

Example: I <u>was reading</u> a book **while** my brother <u>was watching</u> TV.

was playing	*play:* I _____ football	while	*play:* my sister _____ tennis.	was playing
was talking	*talk:* She _____ to a friend	while	*sleep:* he _____ on the sofa.	was sleeping
were swimming	*swim:* They _____ in the pool	while	*rain:* it _____.	was raining
was cleaning	*clean:* I _____ the kitchen	while	*clean:* they _____ the bathroom.	were cleaning
was doing	*do:* My brother _____ his homework	while	*take:* we _____ the dog for a walk.	were taking

b) I was reading a book **when** my mum came in.

> Das Past Progressive verwendest du auch um auszudrücken, dass **eine Handlung andauerte, als etwas anderes begann** bzw. geschah.

Example: I <u>was reading</u> a book **when** my brother <u>came in</u>.

was playing	*play:* I _____ football	when	*start:* it _____ to rain.	started
was talking	*talk:* She _____ to a friend	when	*call:* her mother _____ her.	called
were swimming	*swim:* They _____ in the pool	when	*begin:* the storm _____.	began
were waiting	*wait:* We _____ at the bus stop	when	*arrive:* the bus _____.	arrived

Simple Past and Past Progressive

a)

I was reading a book

while

my brother was watching TV.

*Das Past Progressive verwendest du auch um auszudrücken, dass in der Vergangenheit **zwei Handlungen zur gleichen Zeit** abliefen.*

Choose a verb from the verb box and fill in the Past Progressive!

Example: I <u>was reading</u> a book   while   my brother <u>was reading</u> a comic.

		cut – play – ride – clean		
was playing	I _____ football	while	my sister _____ tennis.	was playing
was cleaning	She _____ the bedroom	while	he _____ the kitchen.	was cleaning
were riding	They _____ their bikes	while	Tina _____ her horse.	was riding
was cutting	I _____ the tomatoes	while	they _____ the onions.	were cutting

b)

I was reading a book **when** my mum came in.

*Das Past Progressive verwendest du auch um auszudrücken, dass **eine Handlung andauerte, als etwas anderes begann bzw. geschah**.*

Choose a verb from the verb box and fill in the Past Progressive and the Simple Past!

Example: I <u>was reading</u> a book   when   my brother <u>came in</u>.

		wait – swim – read – sleep		come – start – arrive – open	
was swimming	I _____ in the pool	when	it _____ to rain.	started
was sleeping	She _____ in her bed	when	her mother _____ into her room.	came
was reading	He _____ a book	when	his friend _____ the door.	opened
were waiting	We _____ at the bus stop	when	the bus _____.	arrived

Adverbs and Adjectives

	Adjective	→	Adverb	add "-ly"
	beautiful	ly	sing beautiful-**ly**	
a) two consonants + "e" at the end		→		**leave out the "e"**
	terri**ble**	~~e~~ ly	play terri**bly**	
b) "y" at the end		→		**change "y" to "i"**
	hungr**y**	ily	eat hungr**ily**	
c) "ic" at the end		→		**add "-ally"**
	fantast**ic**	ally	act fantastic**ally**	

a) Write down the correct adverb form!

Example: quick: He runs _____. → He runs <u>quickly</u>.
nice: She sings _____. → She sings <u>nicely</u>.

Fold back!			Fold back!
badly	a) *bad*: He sings _____.	e) *easy*: He is jumping _____.	easily
carefully	b) *careful*: She works _____.	f) *slow*: I always eat _____.	slowly
angrily	c) *angry*: Her father shouted _____.	g) *dramatic*: She acted _____.	dramatically
horribly	d) *horrible*: She cried _____.	h) *sad*: Linda explained it _____.	sadly

adjective ↓ beschreibt ein **Substantiv** bzw. ein **Pronomen** näher	He is a *quick* runner. He is *quick*.	He runs *quickly*. She is *really quick*. She runs *really quickly*.	**adverb** ↓ beschreibt ein **Verb** näher bzw. ein **Adjektiv** oder ein **Adverb**

b) Fill in the adjective and the adverb!

Example: *adjective* — quick: Peter is a *quick* runner
adverb — but Tina *plays quickly*.

Fold back!			Fold back!
beautiful	a) *beautiful*: She is a _____ girl.	But Sarah sings _____.	beautifully
fantastic	b) *fantastic*: I had a _____ match.	I played _____.	fantastically
hungry	c) *hungry*: The cat isn't _____.	But the dog eats _____.	hungrily
terrible	d) *terrible*: This play is _____.	They act _____.	terribly
cheap	e) *cheap*: This is a _____ snack bar.	We can eat _____ here.	cheaply

Adverbs and Adjectives

		Adjective	→	Adverb		add "-ly"
		beautiful	ly	sing beautiful-**ly**		
a)	two consonants + "e" at the end		→			leave out the "e"
		terri~~e~~le	~~e~~ly	play terri**bly**		
b)	"y" at the end		→			change "y" to "i"
		hungr**y**	ily	eat hungr**ily**		
c)	"ic" at the end		→			add "-ally"
		fantastic	ally	act fantastic**ally**		

a) Write down the correct adverb form!

Example: quick: He runs _____. → He runs <u>quickly</u>.
nice: She sings _____. → She sings <u>nicely</u>.

noisily	a) *noisy:* He works _____.	e) *clear:* He speaks _____.	clearly
nervously	b) *nervous:* She is waiting _____.	f) *crazy:* They are dancing _____.	crazily
unusually	c) *unusual:* It is _____ quiet.	g) *terrible:* I am _____ tired.	terribly
aggressively	d) *aggressive:* He shouts _____.	h) *poor:* Sorry, you did _____.	poorly

adjective ↓	He is a *quick* <u>runner</u>. He is *quick*.	He <u>runs</u> *quickly*. She is *really* <u>quick</u>. She <u>runs</u> *really* <u>quickly</u>.	**adverb** ↓
beschreibt ein **Substantiv** bzw. ein **Pronomen** näher			beschreibt ein **Verb** näher bzw. ein **Adjektiv** oder ein **Adverb**

b) Decide for the adjective or the adverb form!

Example: *adjective*   *adverb*
quick: Peter is a <u>quick</u> <u>runner</u>   but Tina <u>plays</u> *quickly*.

bad	a) *bad:* He is a _____ <u>player</u>.	He <u>plays</u> _____!	badly
angrily	b) *angry:* He <u>shouted</u> _____.	<u>He</u> was _____.	angry
quietly	c) *quiet:* Hey! <u>Walk</u> _____!	<u>You</u> must be _____!	quiet
energetically	d) *energetic:* She <u>spoke</u> _____.	That was an _____ <u>presentation</u>.	energetic
beautiful	e) *beautiful:* He has a _____ <u>voice</u>.	They <u>sing</u> _____.	beautifully

Adverbs and Adjectives

	Adjective	→	Adverb	add "-ly"
	beautiful	ly	sing beautiful-**ly**	
a) two consonants + "e" at the end		→		leave out the "e"
	terri**ble**	~~e~~ ly	play terri**bly**	
b) "y" at the end		→		change "y" to "i"
	hungr**y**	ily	eat hungr**ily**	
c) "ic" at the end		→		add "-ally"
	fantast**ic**	ally	act fantastic**ally**	

a) Write down the correct adverb form!

Example: quick: He runs _____. → He runs <u>quickly</u>.
nice: She sings _____. → She sings <u>nicely</u>.

Fold back!			Fold back!
funnily	a) *funny*: She speaks _____.	e) *loud*: They laughed _____.	loudly
fantastically	b) *fantastic*: The team played _____.	f) *strict*: The teacher said it _____.	strictly
carefully	c) *careful*: He was driving _____.	g) *real*: I am _____ sad.	really
busily	d) *busy*: She worked _____.	h) *kind*: She _____ helped the man.	kindly

| **adjective** ↓ beschreibt ein **Substantiv** bzw. ein **Pronomen** näher | He is a <u>quick</u> <u>runner</u>. He is <u>quick</u>. | He <u>runs</u> <u>quickly</u>. She is <u>really</u> <u>quick</u>. She <u>runs</u> <u>really</u> <u>quickly</u>. | **adverb** ↓ beschreibt ein **Verb** näher bzw. ein **Adjektiv** oder ein **Adverb** |

b) Decide for the adjective or the adverb form!

Example: *adjective* — quick: Peter is a <u>quick</u> <u>runner</u> — *adverb* but Tina <u>plays</u> <u>quickly</u>.

Fold back!			Fold back!
slow	a) *slow:* He is a _____ worker.	He works _____!	slowly
happily	b) *happy:* She waved _____.	She was _____.	happy
carefully	c) *careful:* Hey! Walk _____!	You must be _____!	careful
tragically	d) *tragic:* Don died _____.	This was a _____ accident.	tragic
real	e) *real:* This is a _____ story.	They sing _____ nicely.	really
hopeful	f) *hopeful:* She is _____.	See you soon _____!	hopefully

Adverbs – Special forms and spellings – Activity: Sorting

	Adjective	→	Adverb	
				add "-ly"
	beautiful	ly	sing beautifully	
a) two consonants + "e" at the end		→		leave out the "e"
	terrible	ℯ ly	play terribly	
b) "y" at the end		→		change "y" to "i"
	hungry	ily	eat hungrily	
c) "ic" at the end		→		add "-ally"
	fantastic	ally	act fantastically	
d) specials				
	fast	=	fast	(schnell)
	hard	=	hard	(hart)
	high	=	high	
	good		well	(gut)
			hardly	(kaum)

Write down the adjectives into the correct adverb box!
Be careful: There are some adjectives left. These just need a simple -ly for the adverb form.

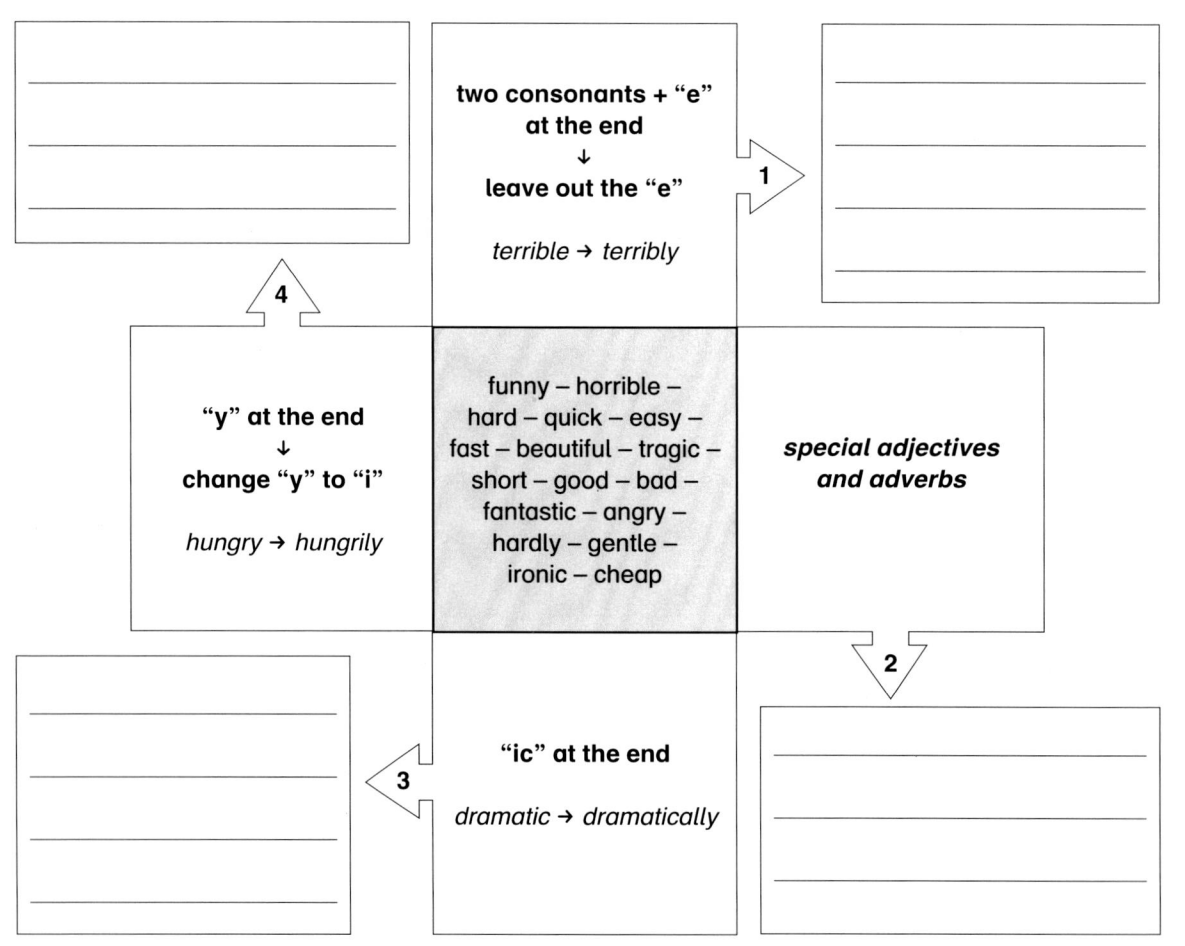

Answers:
1: horrible – horribly / gentle – gently
2: hard – hard / fast – fast / good – well / hardly – hardly
3: tragic – tragically / fantastic – fantastically / ironic – ironically
4: funny – funnily / easy – easily / angry – angrily
Left over: quick – quickly / beautiful – beautifully / short – shortly / bad – badly / cheap – cheaply